one million things

HUMAN BODY

**LONDON, NEW YORK,
MELBOURNE, MUNICH, AND DELHI**

For Tall Tree Ltd.:
Editors Neil Kelly, Claudia Martin, and Jon Richards
Designers Ben Ruocco and Ed Simkins

For Dorling Kindersley:
Senior editor Carron Brown
Senior designer Smiljka Surla

Managing editor Linda Esposito
Managing art editor Diane Thistlethwaite

Commissioned photography Stefan Podhorodecki
Creative retouching Steve Willis

Publishing manager Andrew Macintyre
Category publisher Laura Buller

DK picture researcher Ria Jones
Production editor Andy Hilliard
Production controller Charlotte Oliver

Jacket design Hazel Martin
Jacket editor Matilda Gollon
Design development manager Sophia M. Tampakopoulos Turner
Development team Yumiko Tahata

First published in the United States in 2010 by
DK Publishing,
375 Hudson Street, New York, New York 10014

A catalog catalogue record for this book
is available from the Library of Congress

ISBN: 978-0-75666-288-2

Printed and bound by Leo, China

**Discover more at
www.dk.com**

one million things

HUMAN BODY

Written by:

Richard Walker

 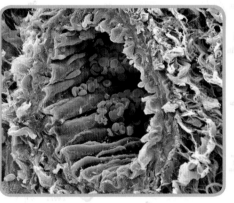

Contents

MADE OF CELLS
These stem cells from a human fetus have real potential. They could become any one of the many types of cells that organize themselves to build and operate a body.

Organization

PEOPLE

From the Arctic to the Amazon rainforest, from New York City to Tokyo, people may appear a little different, but those differences are superficial. Under the skin, our bodies look the same and work in identical ways. What is remarkable, though, is how adaptable we are. Thanks to their initiative and intelligence, people have adapted to a variety of lifestyles in contrasting locations.

▼ INUIT

Experts at survival in the cold of ice and snow, the Inuit have lived in northern Canada and Greenland for about 5,000 years. Well-insulated by thick clothing, traditionally made from fur and hides, they travel across the ice on dogsleds or snowmobiles. The Inuit survive by fishing, catching whales, and hunting caribou.

◀ YANOMAMI

Isolated from the outside world until the 20th century, the Yanomami live in small villages in the hot, humid Amazon rain forest of South America. The Yanomami clear areas of forest to grow bananas and cassava, collect fruit, and hunt for meat and fish. Periodically, they move to new parts of the forest.

BEDOUIN ▶

These desert people of North Africa and Arabia lead a nomadic existence, traveling from oasis to oasis, and living in tents. While many Bedouin have moved to cities, some continue the traditional lifestyle, wearing the clothing shown here to protect them from the intense heat. They use camels, animals that can survive for weeks without water, to transport goods for trade. They also depend on camels for hides, and for meat and milk.

◀ CITY DWELLER

Over three billion people live in cities, with millions more joining them annually. City dwellers depend on food and other resources being brought to them from outside. People come to cities to find opportunities and have a good lifestyle, enjoying the many facilities that cities offer. Cities can also be places of great poverty, where pollution and stress reduce life expectancy.

▼ EUROPEAN FARMER

Farming started some 10,000 years ago in the Middle East. Growing food, rather than hunting or foraging for it, enabled people to settle in small communities. Today, European farmers produce food on a much bigger scale to supply large populations of people, mainly in cities. Using modern techniques, they grow crops and keep animals, such as cattle and sheep. These animals are usually specially bred for maximum yields of meat, milk, or wool.

◄ SAN

The hot, dry Kalahari Desert, which stretches across Botswana and Namibia in southern Africa, is home to the San people. The San are hunter-gathers who lead a nomadic lifestyle, and have done so for thousands of years. They forage in one area of the desert for food and water, living in temporary shelters, before moving on. The men hunt animals, while the women gather berries, nuts, and roots.

▲ BAJAU

The Bajau people of Southeast Asia spend most of their life at sea. They live on boats and stilt houses in the Sulu Sea between the Philippines and Borneo, returning to land only to get fresh water. They depend for their existence on trading and fishing. An important catch for Bajau fishermen is the trepang, a type of sea cucumber (a sluglike relative of starfish) that is prized by the Chinese.

ANCESTORS

In African forests, around seven million years ago, our apelike ancestors started to walk on two legs. Being upright, their hands could perform tasks, and they could spot predators from afar. Over millions of years, evolution equipped hominins (the human line) with bigger brains, the ability to harness fire, make tools, and develop culture.

Face protrudes like that of an ape

AUSTRALOPITHECUS AFARENSIS ▶

This chimp-sized, ancient relative walked on two legs, although probably with hips and knees bent, rather than straight as we do. *Australopithecus afarensis* lived in East Africa between 3.9 and 2.9 million years ago, occupying mixed woodlands and grasslands and feeding on leaves and roots.

◀ AUSTRALOPITHECUS AFRICANUS

Between three and two million years ago, *Australopithecus africanus* lived in the open woodlands of southern Africa. They had a brain a bit bigger than a chimp's, lived in small groups, and fed on fruits, seeds, roots, insects, and, probably, small mammals, much as chimps do today. Although their jaws and teeth were bigger than a modern human's, they are much more similar to ours than to those of an ape.

◀ HOMO HABILIS

Around two-thirds our height, "handy man" (*Homo habilis*) lived in East Africa between 2.5 and 1.6 million years ago, and had flatter faces and significantly bigger brains than their ancestors. They were the first hominins to make and use tools, particularly stone flakes for cutting and scraping meat. They ate much more meat, giving them a diet rich in the nutrients needed to fuel brain expansion.

Hairless skin allowed sweating to take place to cool body

As in chimps, arms are longer than the legs

Hands used to hold and make stone tools

HOMO ERGASTER ▶

"Working man" (*Homo ergaster*) lived between two and 1.3 million years ago, and was probably the first hominin to leave Africa. They had lost the long arms and stoop of earlier hominins, had bigger brains, and were tall, slender, long-legged, and able to run fast and to migrate over long distances. They produced advanced, sophisticated stone tools such as the teardrop-shaped hand axes.

◄ HOMO ERECTUS

"Upright man" (*Homo erectus*) lived between 1.8 million and 50,000 years ago, and migrated from Africa, spreading across Asia. Smarter than earlier hominins, they built the first shelters, took to sea on rafts, and harnessed fire to cook food. In subtropical Asia, they may have used bamboo to make spears or prod prey out of trees. They also hunted in groups to kill larger animals.

Body as upright and athletic as modern humans

Prominent brow ridge overshadows eyes

▼ HOMO HEIDELBERGENSIS

Heidelberg man (*Homo heidelbergensis*) was taller and bigger-brained than *Homo erectus*, but still had big brow ridges and a flat forehead. Possibly a direct ancestor of both Neanderthals and modern humans, they lived in Asia, Africa, and—a first for hominins—Europe between 800,000 and 250,000 years ago. They were not scavengers, but skilled hunters, who, after the kill, butchered deer, rhino, and other prey using stone tools.

This hominin used spears for hunting large prey

Modern humans have a flat face and tall forehead

HOMO SAPIENS ▶

Modern humans (*Homo sapiens*), who evolved some 195,000 years ago in East Africa, had a more slender build and a bigger brain than earlier hominins. They left Africa around 60,000 years ago and spread across the world. About 40,000 years ago, culture, tool use, hunting methods, and language suddenly developed much more rapidly. The invention of agriculture 10,000 years ago allowed humans to settle in cities.

▲ HOMO NEANDERTHALENSIS

The Neanderthals (*Homo neanderthalensis*) lived in Europe and central Asia between 230,000 and 28,000 years ago. Their short, stocky build helped them to survive in a cold climate, and they were very strong. They had a tough existence, often suffering injuries as they hunted big prey, such as bison, using spears and stone axes. Neanderthals were the first hominins to bury their dead.

CELLS

Imagine you could take a tiny sample of body tissue and look at it under a microscope. You would see that it was made up of tiny, living building blocks, called cells. In all, among the 100 trillion cells it takes to build a complete body, there are some 200 different types of cells, each with their own shape, size, and function.

❶ CELL BASICS

Although body cells come in many different shapes and sizes, they all share the same basic parts, as shown by this "typical" cell. The membrane controls what enters and leaves the cell. Floating in the cytoplasm are tiny structures called organelles. Inside the nucleus are the instructions that control all of the cell's activities.

❷ RED BLOOD CELLS

Found in their billions in your blood, these dimpled, disk-shaped cells differ from all other cells in one important way. Red blood cells have no nucleus. Instead, their insides are packed with a red-colored protein called hemoglobin that can pick up and release oxygen. That is why red blood cells are such excellent oxygen carriers.

❸ FAT CELLS

Also called adipose cells, these big, bulky cells are packed with droplets of energy-rich fat. Together, groups of fat cells form adipose tissue. As well as providing an energy store, a layer of adipose tissue under the skin insulates the body and reduces heat loss. It also forms a protective cushion around organs, such as the eyes and kidneys.

Cell membrane surrounds cell

Cytoplasm (a jellylike liquid) fills area between membrane and nucleus

Organelles perform range of life-giving roles, such as releasing energy and making proteins

Nucleus controls cell workings

❹ WHITE BLOOD CELL

Without its white blood cells, the body would be unable to protect itself from pathogens, such as harmful bacteria, that cause disease. White blood cells, such as this lymphocyte, form a key part of the body's immune system. They patrol the bloodstream and tissues, ever ready to destroy invaders.

❽ EPITHELIAL CELLS

Inside the body, every tube (including blood vessels) and cavity (such as the stomach) is lined with tightly packed epithelial cells. Together, they form a sheet of epithelial tissue that covers and protects underlying cells. These pavement epithelial cells, which line the cheeks, are broad and flat.

❾ STEM CELLS

Unlike the other cells described here, stem cells are unspecialized and have no specific job to do. They are, though, still vitally important. Stem cells constantly divide to produce more cells like themselves, some of which turn into specialized cells. In bone marrow, for example, stem cells make millions of blood cells every second to replace those that are worn out.

❺ MUSCLE CELLS

Running for a bus, pushing food along the intestines, and keeping the heart beating are all examples of body movements. All these movements are produced by long cells called muscle fibers. They have the unique ability to contract, or get shorter, to create pulling power. The long skeletal muscle fibers shown here are bound together in muscles that move our bodies.

❻ NERVE CELLS

Neurons, or nerve cells, produce and carry high-speed, electrical signals called nerve impulses. They make up the nervous system, a control network that uses those signals to coordinate most body activities, from thinking to walking. Each neuron consists of a nucleus-containing cell body (center) with many projections that either receive signals from, or transmit signals to, other neurons.

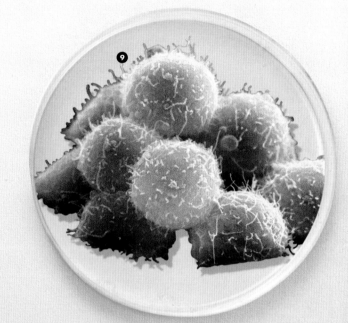

❼ OSTEOCYTES

These spiky bone cells are tasked with maintaining the matrix of fibers and mineral salts that makes up the bulk of bones. Osteocytes live in isolation, each in its own cavity in the bone matrix. They remain in contact with each other, communicating through tiny "threads" that pass along the hairlike canals linking the cavities.

❿ SEX CELLS

One of these male sex cells (sperm) fuses with a female sex cell (egg) to produce a fertilized egg that develops into a new human being. Sperm seek out an egg by swimming toward it. A long tail propels the sperm, and a streamlined head contains half the instructions needed to make a baby. The remaining instructions are inside the egg.

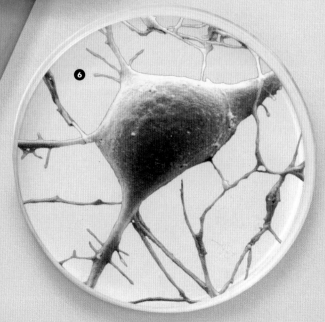

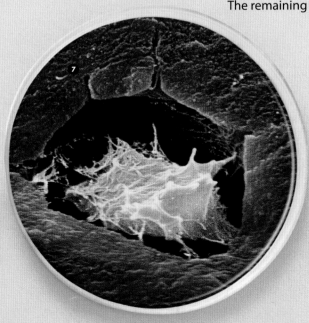

INSTRUCTIONS

The nucleus of a cell is often described as its control center. Inside are 46 chromosomes that contain some 22,000 genes. These genes are built from a remarkable molecule called deoxyribonucleic acid (DNA) that can copy itself and be copied. Genes provide a library of instructions to build an amazingly diverse range of substances called proteins from their building blocks, amino acids. Among many other things, proteins build cells, make their chemical reactions work, carry oxygen, and fight disease. Without proteins, life would be impossible.

❶ CHROMOSOMES

The nucleus of just about every body cell contains two sets of 23 chromosomes—46 in all. Each chromosome consists of one, very long DNA molecule that contains some of the instructions needed to build and run the cell. Normally, chromosomes are long and stringy, but when a cell is about to divide they shorten and split to form the X-shaped structures you can see here.

Sequence of bases provides "letters" of instructions

❷ DNA

A molecule of DNA resembles a long, twisted ladder, its two strands linked by "rungs" consisting of four types of chemicals called bases. These bases form the "letters" of the coded instructions—genes— required to make specific proteins. Protein production takes place in a cell's cytoplasm, whereas DNA is found in the nucleus. To transfer instructions to the cytoplasm, a gene has to be copied. That is the job of RNA.

❸ RNA

An RNA (ribonucleic acid) molecule is similar to DNA, but is much shorter, has only one strand, and comes in different forms. Messenger RNA (mRNA) copies a short section of DNA instructions—one gene— and moves from the nucleus to the cytoplasm. Here, transfer RNA molecules deliver a selection of 20 different amino acids and line them up precisely, according to the instructions in mRNA, to build a new protein.

Backbone of one DNA strand

❼ HEMOGLOBIN

Red blood cells contain hemoglobin, one of the body's most important transport proteins. Hemoglobin is a complex protein with four subunits, each equipped with a non-protein heme group containing iron. In the lungs, these heme groups pick up oxygen molecules and carry them to every cell in the body. Without this oxygen, cells would not be able to release any energy.

❽ ANTIBODIES

These Y-shaped proteins play a key role in the immune system, defending the body against infection by disease-causing pathogens. When invading pathogens are detected by defence cells called B lymphocytes, they immediately start multiplying to set up an antibody production factory. This churns out masses of antibody molecules that travel in blood and lymph, and stick onto and disable specific pathogens so they can be destroyed.

❹ COLLAGEN

The most common protein in the body, collagen takes the form of tough fibers. Collagen fibers give support and strength to tendons and other connective tissues, and prevent more delicate tissues from tearing apart. Another, more rubbery type of fiber, called elastin, allows connective tissue, such as that in the skin, to stretch and bounce back. Together, collagen and elastin, along with the protein keratin in hair and nails, are called structural proteins, and they play a key role in body construction.

❺ MEMBRANE PROTEINS

The fatty membrane that surrounds every cell contains several different types of protein. Some run through the membrane and act as channels through which small molecules can enter or leave the cell. Other proteins, in the outer part of the membrane, act as receptors to which chemical messengers, such as hormones, can bind. Finally, a third type of protein projects outward from a cell's surface. These markers identify the cell so that it can be recognized by other cells.

❻ ENZYMES

Cells are alive because of the chemical reactions—known collectively as metabolism—happening inside them. These reactions either break down fuels to release energy, or use energy to build new substances. However, without a group of proteins called enzymes, none of this would be possible. Enzymes, such as aconitase shown here, are biological catalysts that speed up the rate of chemical reactions to make metabolism happen.

MULTIPLICATION

Each one of us started life as a fertilized egg. That single cell gave rise to the trillions of cells that make up the body by a process of multiplication called cell division, or mitosis. The nucleus of every cell contains 23 pairs of threadlike chromosomes that hold the instructions for life. During mitosis, as shown here, chromosomes are duplicated and separated into two new identical cells. As well as enabling us to grow and develop, mitosis produces billions of new cells every day that are used to repair and maintain the body.

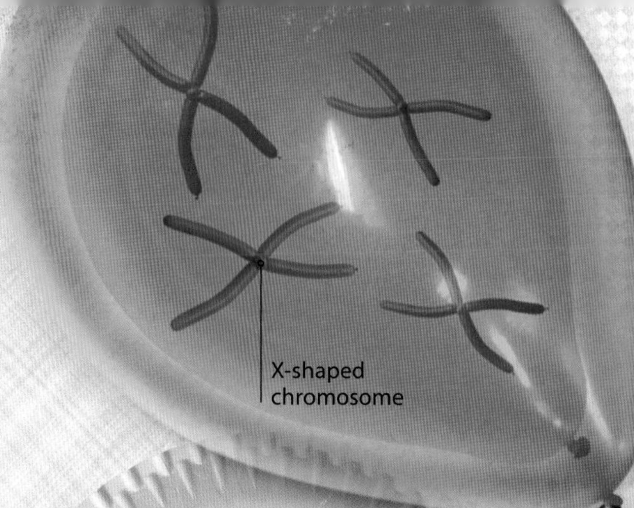

X-shaped chromosome

▲ PREPARATION
Inside a cell nucleus, each chromosome starts the cell division process by shortening, thickening, and making a copy of itself. The two copies, called chromatids, are held together at the "waist" to form an X-shaped structure. Here, for simplicity's sake, only two pairs of chromosomes are shown. One member of each pair came originally from the mother (red), and one from the father (blue).

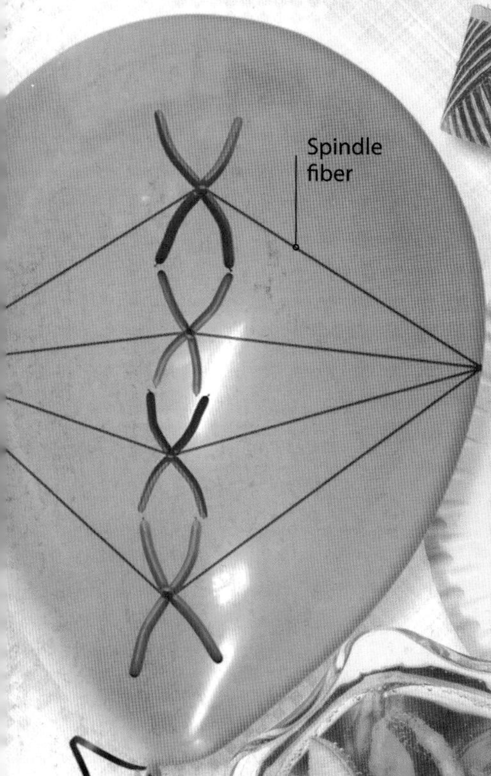

Spindle fiber

◄ LINING UP
The membrane surrounding the cell's nucleus disappears. At the same time, a framework of tiny fibers, called the spindle, appears in the cell's cytoplasm. The chromosomes line up across the equator, or center, of the cell. The tips of spindle fibers attach themselves to the "waist" of each chromosome in readiness for the next stage of mitosis.

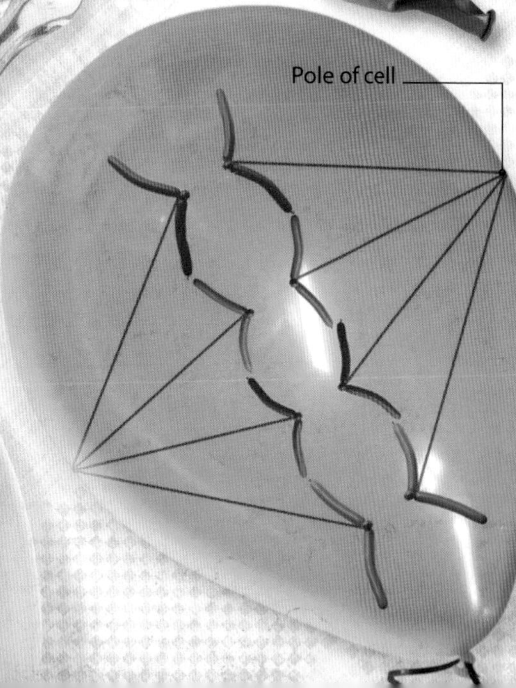

Pole of cell

◄ SEPARATION
It's now time for the two identical chromatids that make up each chromosome to part company. The tiny structure that grips the chromatids together at the "waist" splits. The spindle fibers attached to the chromosomes now start to get shorter. As they do so, they pull "sister" chromatids apart from each other towards the ends, or poles, of the cell.

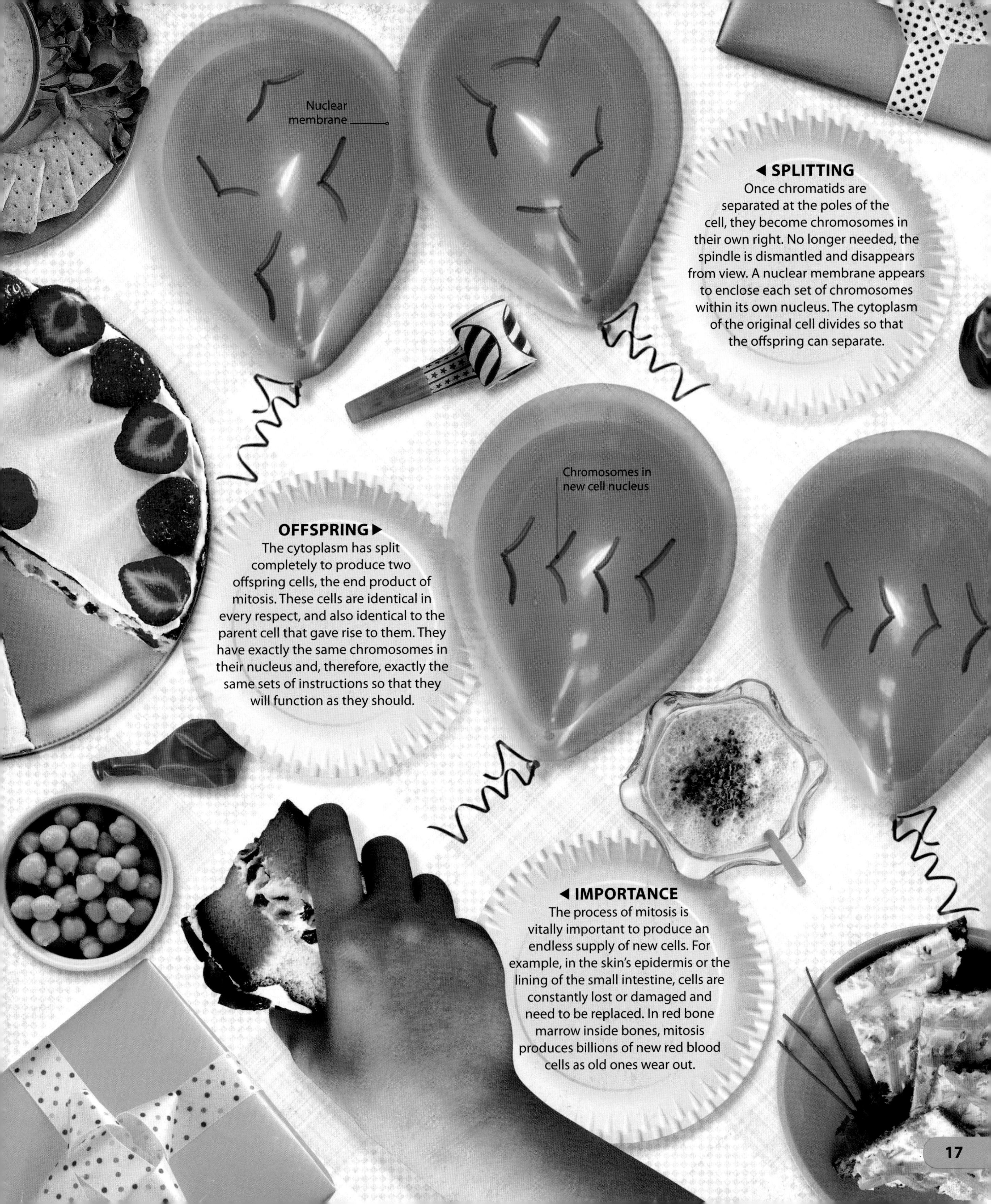

Nuclear
membrane

◄ SPLITTING
Once chromatids are
separated at the poles of the
cell, they become chromosomes in
their own right. No longer needed, the
spindle is dismantled and disappears
from view. A nuclear membrane appears
to enclose each set of chromosomes
within its own nucleus. The cytoplasm
of the original cell divides so that
the offspring can separate.

Chromosomes in
new cell nucleus

OFFSPRING ►
The cytoplasm has split
completely to produce two
offspring cells, the end product of
mitosis. These cells are identical in
every respect, and also identical to the
parent cell that gave rise to them. They
have exactly the same chromosomes in
their nucleus and, therefore, exactly the
same sets of instructions so that they
will function as they should.

◄ IMPORTANCE
The process of mitosis is
vitally important to produce an
endless supply of new cells. For
example, in the skin's epidermis or the
lining of the small intestine, cells are
constantly lost or damaged and
need to be replaced. In red bone
marrow inside bones, mitosis
produces billions of new red blood
cells as old ones wear out.

17

ORGANS

The heart, brain, and kidneys are all familiar body organs, each with their own specific jobs—but what are they made from? Each organ is constructed from two or more types of tissues that work together to make the organ function. There are four main kinds of tissues in the body. Put simply, epithelial tissues cover, connective tissues support, muscular tissues move, and nervous tissues control. Each tissue is a community of the same or similar types of cells.

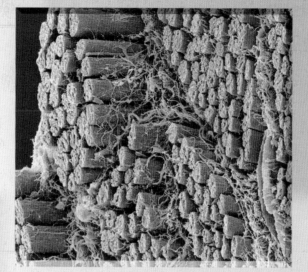

▼ EPITHELIAL TISSUE

Also called epithelium, epithelial tissue consists of sheets of tightly packed cells that form the inner linings of hollow organs and cavities including the stomach and blood vessels. Epithelial tissue, as shown here, also forms the epidermis, the upper layer of skin. The epithelium protects the tissues beneath it from pathogens or harmful substances. Epithelial cells divide continually to provide replacements for those that are worn away or damaged.

▼ MUSCLE TISSUE

Like other types of muscle tissue, the smooth muscle tissue shown here makes movement. It is made of muscle fibers that use energy to shorten and create a pulling force. For example, smooth muscle fibers in the walls of the bladder squeeze urine out of the body. Skeletal muscle tissue moves the skeleton, while cardiac muscle tissue makes the heart beat.

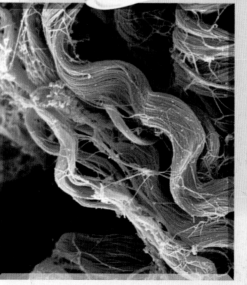

▲ CONNECTIVE TISSUE

There are several different types of these tissues in the body. Many connective tissues, as their name suggests, support and protect other tissues and bind them together. These collagen fibers, found between connective tissue cells, provide strength and flexibility. Bone and cartilage are also connective tissues, as are adipose tissue and blood. They also form tendons and ligaments.

Brain controls most body activities, including thinking

Deltoid muscle moves the arm in several directions

Humerus is one of 206 bones that support the body

Lung transfers oxygen from the air to the bloodstream

Heart pumps blood around the body

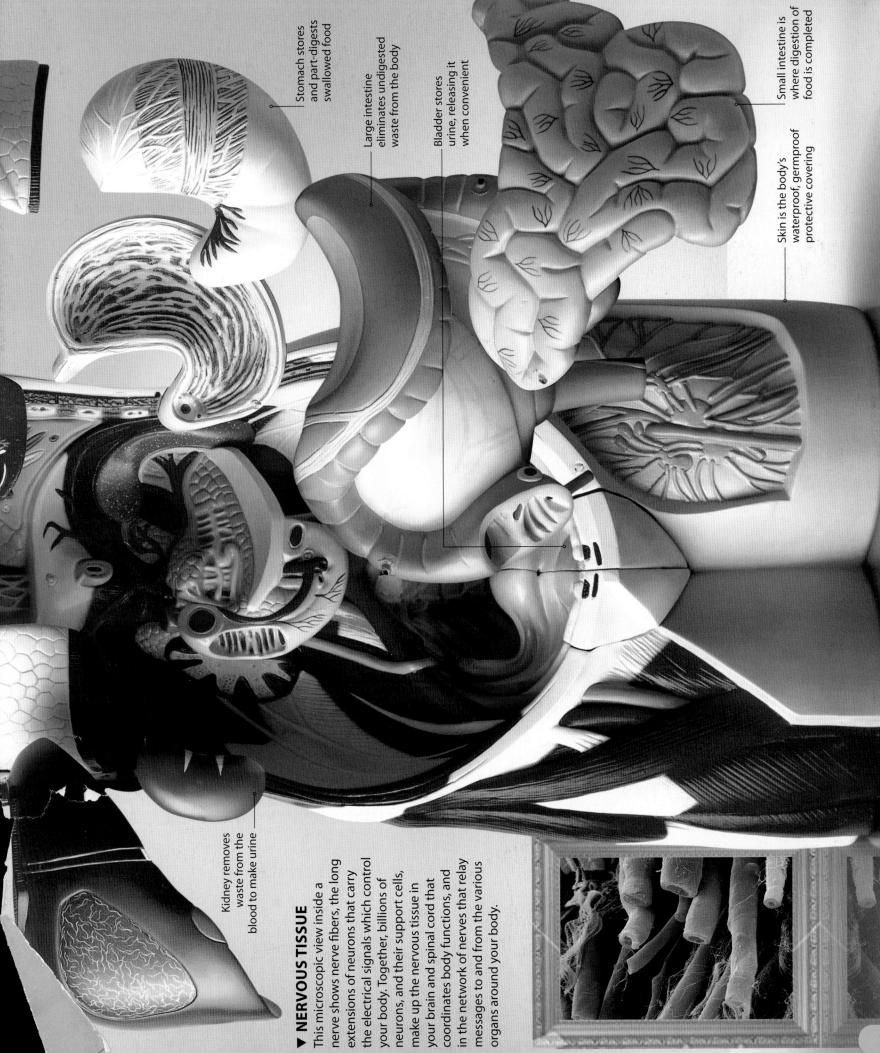

Stomach stores and part-digests swallowed food

Large intestine eliminates undigested waste from the body

Bladder stores urine, releasing it when convenient

Small intestine is where digestion of food is completed

Skin is the body's waterproof, germproof protective covering

Kidney removes waste from the blood to make urine

▼ **NERVOUS TISSUE**
This microscopic view inside a nerve shows nerve fibers, the long extensions of neurons that carry the electrical signals which control your body. Together, billions of neurons, and their support cells, make up the nervous tissue in your brain and spinal cord that coordinates body functions, and in the network of nerves that relay messages to and from the various organs around your body.

SYSTEMS

A total of 12 systems work together to make the human body work. Each system consists of a collection of organs that cooperate to carry out a particular function or functions. For example, the organs making up the digestive system dismantle complex molecules in food to release usable substances, such as glucose or amino acids, that are utilized by body cells to supply energy or build structures.

❶ **Circulatory system** The heart, blood, and blood vessels make up the circulatory or cardiovascular system. Its primary role is to pump blood around the body to supply cells with oxygen, food, and other essentials, and to remove wastes.

❷ **Digestive system** This long canal, including the stomach and intestines, extends from the mouth to the anus. It breaks down food to release essential nutrients that are absorbed into the bloodstream, and disposes of any waste.

❸ **Endocrine system** Like the nervous system, the endocrine system controls body activities. Its glands release chemical messengers, called hormones, into the bloodstream. Hormones target tissues to change their activities and control processes, such as growth.

❹ **Skeletal system** This framework of bones, cartilage, and ligaments supports the body. Flexible joints between bones allow the body to move when muscles anchored to those bones pull them. The skeleton also protects delicate organs, such as the brain, and makes blood cells.

❺ **Reproductive system** The only system that differs between males and females, the reproductive system enables humans to reproduce to create children who will succeed them when they die. Male and female systems each produce sex cells that fuse to create a baby.

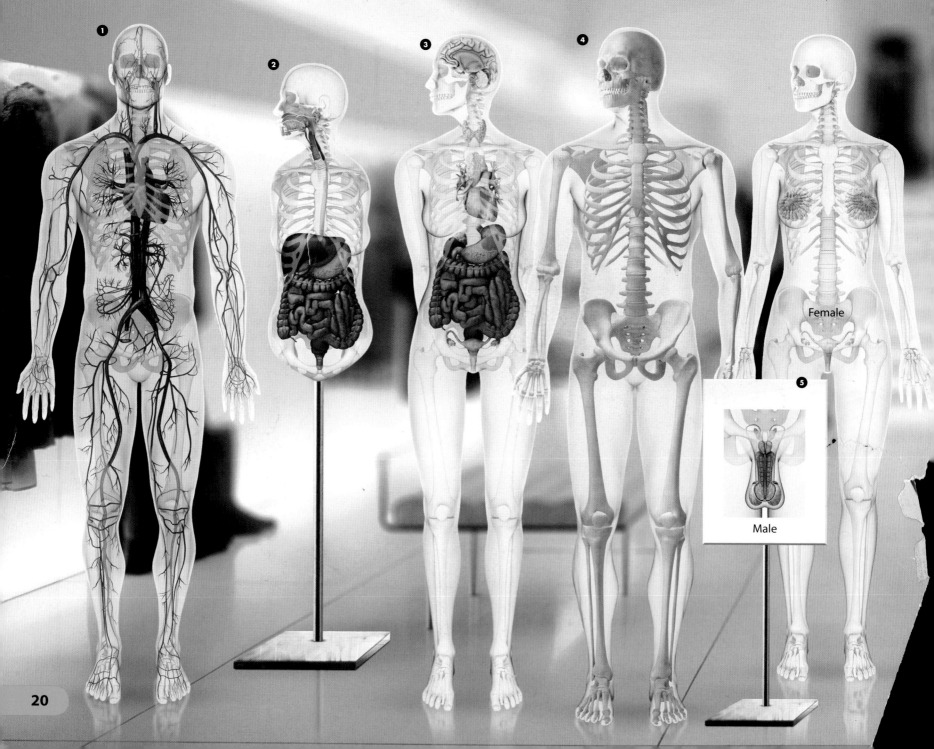

Female

Male

6 Lymphatic system Blood flowing through the tissues leaves excess fluid around tissue cells. This fluid, called lymph, is drained by lymph vessels and returned to the bloodstream. Lymph vessels and nodes make up the lymphatic system.

7 Integumentary system Consisting of the skin, hair, and nails, this system covers the body, preventing the entry of germs and loss of water. It also intercepts harmful rays in sunlight, controls body temperature, and acts as a sense organ.

8 Muscular system The skeletal muscles that cover, and are attached to, the skeleton, create pulling forces that enable us to move. Other types of muscles inside the body push food along the intestine and make the heart beat.

9 Nervous system The body's primary control system, the nervous system uses electrical signals for messages. At its core are the brain and spinal cord. These receive, process, and send information along nerves.

10 Respiratory system Energy is essential for the body and its cells to stay alive. Eating provides energy-rich food. The respiratory system—the airways and lungs—gets oxygen into the body to "burn" these foods to release energy.

11 Urinary system The urinary system removes excess water and wastes from the blood. The kidneys filter blood, mixing water and wastes to make urine, a liquid that is stored in the bladder and then expelled from the body.

12 Immune system This is a lymphocyte, one of the cells that make up the immune system, which destroys harmful bacteria and viruses. Immune system cells are found in the circulatory and lymphatic systems, and in other tissues.

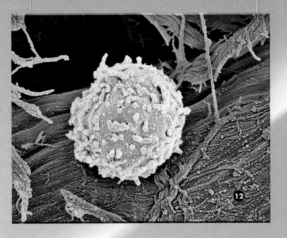

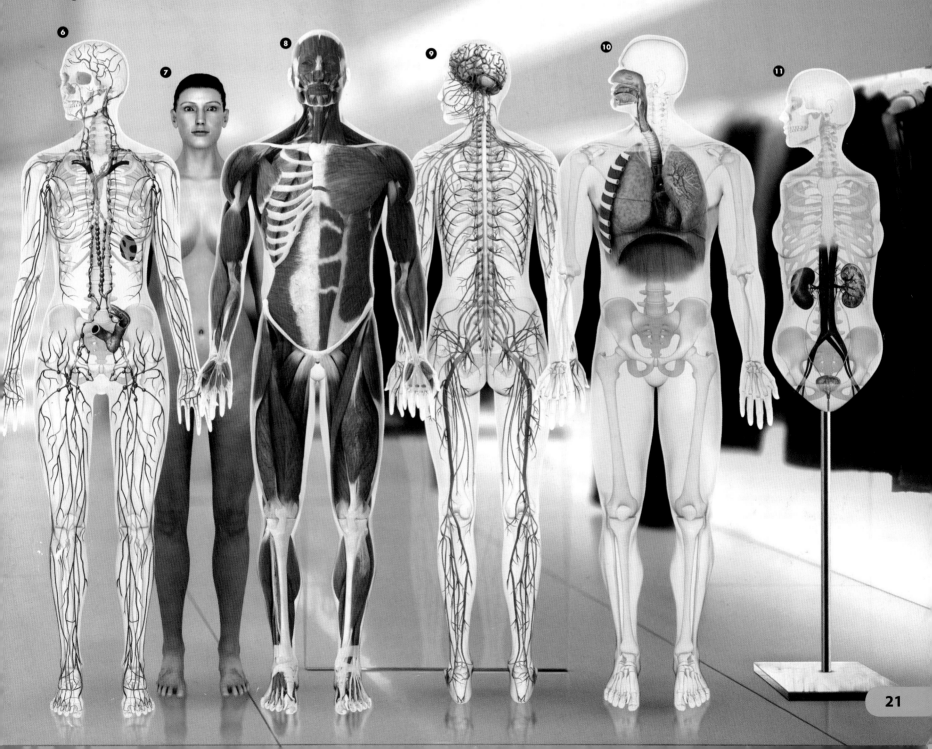

21

LIVING IMAGES

In the past the only way to look inside the living body was to cut it open. In 1895, X rays were discovered, providing a way of imaging the body's insides from the outside. Today, doctors have access to many imaging techniques that help them to diagnose disease so they can start treatment quickly. Many techniques use computers to produce clear, precise images of not just bones—as early X rays did—but of soft tissues and organs as well.

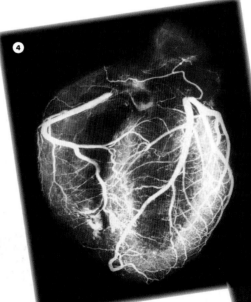

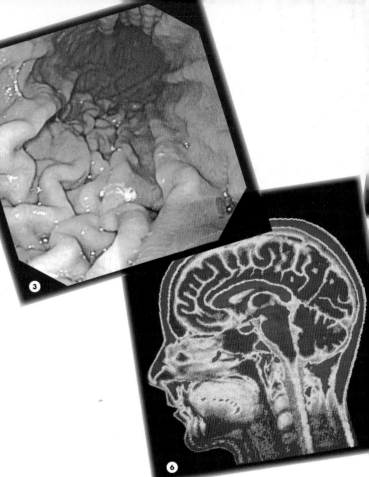

❶ X RAYS

By projecting this high-energy radiation through the body onto a photographic film, a shadow image, or X ray, is produced. Denser tissues, such as bone, absorb X rays and appear pale, while softer tissues appear darker. In this X ray, a substance that absorbs X rays has been introduced into the large intestine to make it visible. The red color is false.

❷ ECHOCARDIOGRAM

Doctors who specialize in the heart and circulatory system use echocardiograms to help them diagnose possible problems. The technique uses ultrasound to create two-dimensional slices through the beating heart. These reveal how good the heart is at pumping blood, and whether its chambers and valves are abnormal. They also trace blood flow through the heart.

❻ MRI SCAN

Magnetic Resonance Imaging (MRI) produces high-quality images of soft tissues, such as this section through the brain. A person lying inside a tunnellike MRI scanner is exposed to a powerful magnetic field that causes atoms inside the body to line up and release radio signals. These are analyzed by a computer to create images.

❸ ENDOSCOPY

This shows the inside of a healthy stomach as revealed by a flexible viewing tube called an endoscope. It is inserted through a natural opening—the mouth, in this case—or through an incision in the skin. The endoscope contains optical fibers that carry in light to illuminate the scene, and carry out images that can be seen on screen.

❼ MRA SCAN

This image of the major blood vessels of the chest was produced using Magnetic Resonance Angiography (MRA) scanning. This is a type of MRI scan used by doctors to look for damaged or diseased blood vessels. Often a special dye is injected into blood vessels to make them even clearer.

❹ ANGIOGRAM

In this special type of X ray, an opaque dye is injected into the bloodstream. The dye absorbs X rays, which means the resulting angiogram shows the outlines of blood vessels, and can detect any disease or damage. In this angiogram, you can see the left and right coronary arteries that supply the heart's muscular wall with oxygen and food.

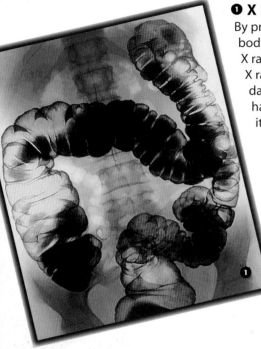

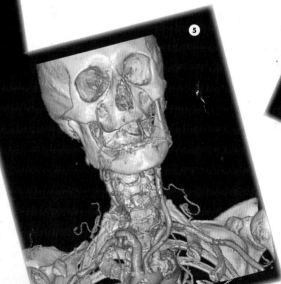

❺ CT SCAN

A Computed Tomography (CT) scanner rotates around a person sending beams of X rays through the body and into a detector linked to a computer. This produces images in the form of "slices" though the body that can be built up into 3-D images, like this one, showing the bones and blood vessels of the upper body.

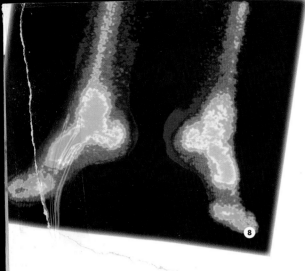

⑩ MEG

A magnetoencephalography (MEG) scan detects magnetic fields, produced by electrical activity of cells in the brain, and converts them into images like this one. This MEG scan shows, as it is happening, the part of the left side of the brain (pink/white) that is sending instructions to muscles to move the right index finger.

⑪ ULTRASOUND

This image shows a 3-D image of a fetus inside its mother. It was produced using high-pitched sound waves called ultrasound. Beamed into the body, they bounce off the fetus' tissues, creating echoes that are turned into images by a computer. The method is very safe because it does not use radiation.

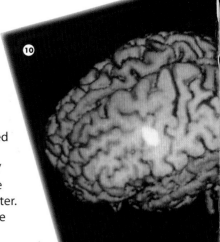

⑧ RADIONUCLIDE

This imaging technique involves injecting a radioactive substance, called a radionuclide, into a body, where it is taken up by bones, in this case the ankles and feet. Here, the radionuclide gives off gamma rays that are detected by a special camera, which converts them into color-coded images. These indicate where cells are most active and, possibly, abnormal.

⑨ PET SCAN

Positron Emission Tomography (PET) scans reveal which parts of the brain are active. When a person is given some special radioactive glucose, brain cells use it to supply energy, releasing particles that are detected by the scanner. This creates an image that is color-coded to show which brain areas are most active.

SKIN

Weighing in at around 11 lbs (5 kg), the skin is our body's biggest organ. Skin acts as a germproof, waterproof overcoat, providing a protective barrier between the body's delicate tissues and our harsh, constantly changing surroundings. Our skin also helps us maintain a constant body temperature of 98.6°F (37°C); filters out harmful rays in sunlight; senses touch, warmth, cold, and pain; and makes vitamin D, a substance that's essential for healthy bones.

▶ SKIN LAYERS

As this section shows, skin has two interlocked layers. The upper, protective epidermis consists mainly of flattened cells that are packed with a tough, waterproof protein called keratin. These cells are continually replaced as they are worn away as skin flakes. The thicker dermis is strong and flexible. It contains blood vessels, sweat glands, and touch sensors, as well as hair follicles. Subcutaneous fat under the dermis insulates the body and stores energy.

Epidermis

Hair in follicle

Blood vessel

Dermis

Nerve

Subcutaneous fat

▼ SKIN COLOR

Human skin color ranges from pale pink through various shades of brown to almost black. Although blood flowing through the dermis gives it pinkness, skin color depends mainly on a brown-black pigment called melanin. This is made and released by cells in the lower epidermis. We all have roughly the same number of these cells, but they produce more melanin in people with darker skin.

▶ SUN PROTECTION

Whether it is pale, dark, or in-between, skin exposed to sunlight for a time gets darker, producing a suntan. That's because sunlight stimulates cells in the skin's epidermis to increase production of melanin. Melanin provides a screen that absorbs harmful ultraviolet rays in sunlight that can damage skin cells. However, in strong sunlight, hats, loose clothing, and suntan lotions are essential to provide extra protection.

▼ NAILS

Imagine how difficult it would be to pick up tiny objects without the benefit of fingernails. These hard, nearly transparent plates also protect and support our sensitive fingertips. Each nail grows from living cells at its base. As these cells divide, their offspring push forward and—just like hairs—fill with tough keratin, harden, and die.

Nails cover fingertips and allow us to scratch itches

Sweat droplet on the ridged skin of a fingertip

Goosebumps appear on the skin when we are cold

▲ SWEAT

This magnified view of a fingertip shows sweat droplets emerging from some of the body's 2.5 million sweat pores. Made by sweat glands in the dermis, sweat is 99 percent water, with a dash of unwanted substances. Sweat glands release extra sweat onto the skin's surface when the body is hot. The sweat evaporates, drawing heat from the body and cooling it down.

▲ GOOSEBUMPS

When we get cold, little pimples called goosebumps appear on our skin. As body temperature falls, tiny muscles automatically pull body hairs upright, at the same time lifting the skin into goosebumps. In furry animals, but not in humans, this action produces a layer of trapped air between hairs and skin that creates a "blanket" to help keep the body warm.

HAIR

We may not have the luxuriant fur of our mammal relatives, but our skin is still covered with millions of hairs. Most of those on the body are short, fine vellus hairs that, when tweaked by visiting insects, warn us that we might be bitten or stung. Thicker, longer terminal hairs are found on the head, eyebrows, and eyelashes. Head hair is protective and also forms an important part of our appearance. Eyebrows and eyelashes both help to protect the eyes. In men, terminal hairs also grow on the face and chest.

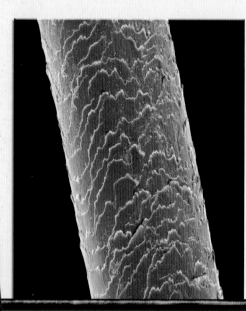

◄ FLEXIBLE FILAMENTS

Hair grows from just about every part of the skin apart from the lips, palms, soles, and nipples. Each hair is a bendy filament of dead, flattened cells arranged in layers around a central core. The outermost layer, the cuticle (left), consists of cells that overlap like tiles on a roof. The shaft is the section of a hair that is visible above the skin's surface. The hair's root lies invisible below the skin's surface.

▼ HAIR CUT

This microscopic view of the skin on a man's face shows beard hairs that have been cut by a razor during shaving, but have continued to grow from their follicles. The cells packing the shafts of the beard hairs are dead, so having a shave is painless—unless the skin is cut! The same is true of getting a hair cut to control, shape, and even to show off the hair on your head.

GROWING HAIRS ▼

Each of the hairs on your body grows from a follicle, a narrow pit deep in the skin's surface. Living cells at the bottom of the follicle divide constantly to make a new hair and push it toward the surface. As the cells move upward, they die because they fill up with keratin, a protein that makes the hair tough and durable. Sebaceous glands release oily sebum into the hair follicles to soften and lubricate the hairs.

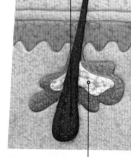

Hair follicle

Sebaceous gland

◀ HEAD OF HAIR

More than 100,000 long, terminal hairs grow from the scalp, the skin that covers the dome of the head. Each head hair grows for several years, at a rate of about 0.4 in (10 mm) per month. It then rests before being pushed out from its follicle by a new hair. Around 100 scalp hairs are lost and replaced each day. Head hair helps keep the head warm and also protects the scalp from harmful ultraviolet rays in sunlight.

▲ HAIR COLOR

Your hair is colored by a pigment called melanin, which comes in four versions—yellow, rust-colored, brown, and black. The version or versions of melanin you have, and the amounts of each, determine whether you have blond, red, brown, or black hair. As people age, melanin production decreases, and their hair gradually turns gray.

▲ GOING BALD

By their 30s, more than a quarter of men have started to go bald. Called male pattern baldness, this loss of hair happens because hair growth in follicles is affected by male sex hormones. Scalp hairs become short and fine, growing for just weeks, before falling out. Over several years, hair is lost first from the temples and then from the top of the head.

◀ STRAIGHT, WAVY, OR CURLY?

Whether your hair is straight, wavy, or curly depends on the shape of your scalp hairs. In cross section, the shaft of straight hair is round, that of wavy hair is oval, while a curly hair shaft is flat. This, in turn, depends on whether the hair is growing from a follicle that is round, oval, or flat in section because the follicle's shape "molds" that of the shaft. In addition, fine hairs grow from narrow follicles, while coarse hairs grow from wide ones.

Straight hair

Wavy hair

Curly hair

PASSENGERS

Unknowingly we are carrying on our skin a variety of, mainly microscopic, passengers. Most are parasites that feed on our skin cells, secretions, or blood. Everyone, without exception, has billions of bacteria on their skin. Many of us are home to tiny eyelash mites, distant cousins of spiders. Less common are other types of mites and their relatives, the ticks. Children often become infected with small insects called head lice. Another blood-feeding insect, the human flea, is much rarer. Other hangers-on include fungi and leeches.

❶ BACTERIA

Billions of bacteria live on the skin's surface, especially in darker, damper places, such as armpits. These bacteria are generally harmless, unless the skin is cut and they get inside the body. *Staphylococcus aureus* (shown here) is found on the skin and can multiply inside hair follicles and cause spots.

❷ EYELASH MITES

Most people, especially those who are older, have these harmless, sausage-shaped mites. Eyelash mites squeeze their long body, head downward, into the hair follicles from which eyelashes grow. Here, they feed on dead skin cells and oily secretions so efficiently that they do not produce any droppings. Mites may emerge at night, though, and take a walk around.

❸ FUNGI

Athlete's foot, an itchy flaking of skin between the toes, is a common complaint. So is ringworm, which causes irritating patches on the skin. Both are caused by fungi, which consist of long filaments that feed on skin cells. They produce fruiting bodies (the cylindrical shapes shown here) that release spores to spread the fungi.

❹ LEECHES

These freshwater relatives of earthworms are expert bloodsuckers. Leeches clamp onto the skin using a powerful sucker surrounding the mouth. Three bladelike jaws then slice painlessly through the skin. Blood is pumped into the leech's body, aided by anticlotting chemicals in its saliva that keep blood flowing freely.

❺ FLEAS

A human flea has sharp mouthparts to pierce the skin and suck blood, a process that causes itching. Once they have fed, these tiny insects do not hang around. Unable to fly, they use their powerful hind legs to jump from person to person, a leap equivalent to us vaulting over a tall building.

❻ HEAD LICE

Gripping a head hair with its curved claws, this head louse is unlikely to be combed or washed away. Neither are its eggs, called nits, that are firmly "glued" onto hair shafts. To feed, head lice descend onto the scalp, pierce the skin, and suck blood. The wingless insects spread easily between children when their heads touch.

❼ CHIGGERS

The eight-legged, plant-feeding harvest mite is harmless, but this chigger, its microscopic six-legged larva, can be a real pest. Picked up by people walking through long grass, chiggers push their heads into hair follicles in the skin. Here, they release a fluid that turns skin cells into a liquid food that can be sucked up. This causes lots of itchy red pimples on the skin.

❽ SCABIES MITES

Also known as itch mites, these tiny scabies mites are pictured here in human skin. After mating, female mites burrow into the skin where they lay eggs that hatch into larval mites which pass easily from person to person. The presence in the skin of burrows, larvae, saliva, and droppings produces an unbearable itching called scabies.

❾ TICK

Bloated with blood, this tick has just detached itself from its host to digest its meal. Ticks pierce the skin of humans, and other animals, using special mouthparts that hold them in place for days. Firmly attached, the tick swells enormously as it sucks blood.

LIFE STORY

Every person, provided they have a normal lifespan, follows the same sequence of mental and physical changes from infancy to old age. Our life story includes rapid development and learning as an infant and child. Then, the great changes of adolescence during the teenage years, when we switch from being children to adults. As adults, we mature before starting to age and "slow down."

❶ INFANT

During the first year of life, infant humans grow rapidly in height and weight, although they are dependent on parents for care, food, and protection. As their muscles and bones grow, infants begin to grasp objects, chew, and crawl, and, by about 12 months old, start to walk. As their brains develop, infants understand simple commands and speak their first words.

❷ CHILD

Childhood extends from infancy to the early teens. Growth is more gradual than in infancy, but this is a time when new skills and knowledge are rapidly acquired. Children develop social skills, become more self-disciplined and able to understand others, learn how to speak fluently and to read and write, and develop the ability to run and play games.

❸ TEENAGER

Adolescence is a time when the body, behavior, and emotions change dramatically. Most obvious are the physical changes, called puberty. These changes are triggered by hormones and start in girls between 10 and 12, and in boys between 12 and 14. Girls grow rapidly and develop a womanly shape. Boys also have a growth spurt and become broader and more muscular.

❹ YOUNG ADULT

The 20s and 30s mark a time in the life story when the body is fully developed and people reach peak fitness and health. Young adulthood is also when we achieve real independence for the first time, can travel and make friends, but also have to take career decisions and make a living. It is also a time of peak fertility when people often form relationships and start families.

❺ MIDDLE AGE

In the 40s and 50s, the body is mature but working well, especially if regular exercise started in young adulthood is maintained. However, the first signs of aging are starting to appear. The ability to think and reason has reached its peak, and years of experience have given individuals the wisdom to make decisions. Children are growing up and are ready to leave home.

❻ OLD AGE

From the early 60s onward, the signs of aging become obvious. Vision and hearing are less efficient, the skin becomes less elastic and wrinkles, and hair thins and turns gray. Joints may be stiffer and bones can become brittle and more likely to break. People are more prone to diseases such as cancers and heart problems. However, many effects of aging can be lessened by a balanced diet and exercise.

REPRODUCTION

Whatever our external appearance and differences, our bodies are all constructed in exactly the same way. The only exceptions are our reproductive systems that divide us into two groups—male and female. Both systems produce sex cells that enable adults to produce offspring that will replace us as we age and die at the end of our natural life span. The male system makes sex cells called sperm, while the female system produces ova (one is called an ovum). When sperm and ova meet, they fuse to produce a new human being.

▼ FEMALE REPRODUCTIVE SYSTEM

Inside a woman's body, the two primary sex organs, the ovaries, are each linked by a fallopian tube to the uterus. At its lower end, the uterus opens to the outside through the vagina. Each month, one ovary releases an ovum that travels along the fallopian tube and, if fertilized by a sperm, settles in the lining of the uterus and develops into a baby. At birth, the baby is pushed out through the vagina.

Uterus protects and nourishes the developing baby

Fallopian tube carries egg to uterus

Ovary contains ova at various stages of maturation

Cervix is a narrow opening that leads into the uterus

Ductus deferens carries sperm to the penis

Urethra, in the penis, also carries urine from the bladder

Vagina receives sperm and is also the canal through which a baby is born

◀ MALE REPRODUCTIVE SYSTEM

A man's primary sex organs, the two testes, make sperm. Sperm production works best at just below normal body temperature, so the testes hang outside the body where it's cooler. A long, curving tube, called the ductus deferens, links each testis to the urethra, which runs along the penis to its tip. During sexual intercourse, the ductus deferens delivers sperm to the urethra. The man's penis then releases sperm from its tip into his partner's vagina.

Testes produce nearly 3,000 sperm per second

◀ OVARIES

When a girl is born, her ovaries contain a lifetime's supply of thousands of immature ova. After puberty, several ova mature each month, but just one bursts out of the ovary and is carried to the uterus. At the same time, the lining of the uterus thickens to receive the ovum should it be fertilized by a sperm. Usually that doesn't happen, and the blood-rich lining is shed through the vagina during a period.

Fringe-like fimbriae surround ovary and transfer ova to fallopian tube

Epididymis stores sperm

Fallopian tube

Efferent duct

TESTES ▶

Inside a testis, sperm are made within tiny, coiled tubes, called seminiferous tubules, that, if unraveled, would extend over 1,650 ft (500 m). From puberty onward, around 250 million sperm are produced here each day. Immature sperm then pass along efferent ducts into the epididymis. Here, they are stored for three weeks while they mature and start to move. They are then pushed into the ductus deferens.

▼ MALE SEX CELLS

Once the male reproductive system is "switched on" at puberty, its testes produce sperm. Sperm, like ova, are produced by a type of cell division called meiosis. This makes cells that have 23 chromosomes, half the normal number. As a result, when a sperm meets an ovum at fertilization, they combine their 23 chromosomes to restore the normal complement of 46.

Seminiferous tubules within testes

Long, whiplike tail enables sperm to swim

◀ FEMALE SEX CELLS

Ova, or eggs, are the female sex cells. Unlike sperm that are released in their millions, ova are released singly each month between puberty, in the early teens, and the menopause. This is the time when a woman can no longer become pregnant, normally in her early fifties. Ova are big cells that cannot, like sperm, move actively. Like sperm, however, they contain just 23 chromosomes.

Ovum, the body's widest cell, is 0.004 in (0.1 mm) across

FERTILIZATION

In order to make a new human life, a sperm must fuse with an ovum. This action, called fertilization, creates a fertilized egg with a full complement of chromosomes—half from the father and half from the mother. Within days a tiny sphere of cells derived from that fertilized egg has arrived and implanted in the uterus, where it will develop and grow into a baby. This first part of pregnancy, which begins with fertilization and ends with implantation, is called conception.

❶ SPERM

These streamlined male sex cells are perfectly adapted to their role of carrying genetic information. Each sperm has a flattened head, a neck (pink), and a long flagellum, or tail. The head carries a payload of 23 chromosomes, the tail beats from side to side to push the sperm through the female reproductive system towards an ovum, and the neck generates the energy to power the tail.

❷ OVUM

Also called an egg, the ovum is spherical, much larger than a sperm, and cannot move on its own. It is surrounded by a zona pellucida, a thick layer outside its cell membrane. The nucleus of the ovum, like the head of the sperm, contains 23 chromosomes. Once released from an ovary, an ovum must be fertilized within 24 hours.

❸ FALLOPIAN TUBE

This narrow tube receives the ovum after it has been released from the ovary and carries it towards the uterus. Hairlike cilia (green) in the lining of the fallopian tube waft the ovum in the right direction. The fallopian tube is also the location for fertilization. Sperm swim along the tube from the uterus and if they meet an ovum fertilization will take place.

❹ FERTLIZATION

Few sperm survive the journey through the uterus to a fallopian tube. If these survivors encounter an ovum, they cluster around it, releasing enzymes to penetrate the ovum's outer layers. Eventually, a single sperm succeeds, loses its tail, and its head fuses with the ovum's nucleus. Once fertilization has happened, no further sperm can penetrate the ovum.

Genetic information stored within head of sperm

300 million sperm released

10,000 sperm enter the uterus

Up to 3,000 sperm reach top of uterus

Half the sperm enter the correct tube

Zona pellucida

A few hundred sperm reach the ovum

One ovum released every 28 days

CELL DIVISION

The fertilized egg now has a full complement of 46 chromosomes—23 from the sperm and 23 from the ovum—containing the instructions to build a human. By 36 hours after fertilization the fertilized egg has divided into two identical cells (above) by mitosis. As it passes along the fallopian tube, the cells continue to divide every 12 hours.

SETTLING IN UTERUS

Some six days after fertilization the fertilized egg is now a hollow ball of cells called the blastocyst. When this arrives in the uterus, it burrows into the soft, thick lining of the uterus. Here, the blastocyst's inner cells form the embryo, and its outer cells form the placenta, which supplies the embryo with food and oxygen.

④

PREGNANCY

Some seven days after fertilization, the fertilized egg, now a hollow ball of cells, sinks into the thick lining of its mother's uterus and embarks on 38 to 40 weeks of development, known as pregnancy. Nurtured and kept warm within a fluid-filled sac, and protected by the wall of the uterus, the tiny embryo, as it is known at first, rapidly grows. It becomes a recognizably human fetus that, once it reaches full size, is pushed out of its mother's uterus during birth.

WEEK 4

Some four weeks after fertilization, the embryo is pea-sized with a C-shaped body and an emerging head region, although it has a beating heart pumping blood, and its nervous system and vital organs, such as the liver and pancreas, are forming.

WEEK 6

The size of a small grape, the embryo grows—along with the body system that is expanding by developing every essential organ indicated. Its rapid development. Growth is now under development.

The embryo has a head that is forming a face, eyes with the form of paddles—arms, legs take and body system—fing, nose, and mouth. Its rings of pigment and brain.

WEEK 8

Now called a fetus, the developing baby is strawberry-sized and floats in a bag of protective amniotic fluid. The fetus is attached to the mother by an umbilical cord, through which it receives food and oxygen. Recognizably human, it has developing fingers and toes, legs and arms that bend, the fetus bones that are hardening, and kidneys that produce urine.

WEEK 10

Now consisting of billions of cells and bigger than a fertilized egg, the fetus is around 1.6 in (4 cm) long. Inside 500 times bigger the brain is adding 250,000 neurons per minute. The the bulging forehead and their fingers have formed and fingernails are growing.

WEEK 30

This 3-D ultrasound image shows a 30-week-old fetus inside the uterus. Ultrasound is a safe imaging method routinely used to check on a baby's progress. The fetus is around 40 cm (15.7 in) long, and its brain is still growing rapidly. The lungs can now, potentially, breathe air should it be born early.

NEWBORN

Newly arrived in a world of noise and bright lights, the baby is weighed soon after birth as one of a series of tests to check that it is healthy. The newborn has just taken its first breaths and the umbilical cord, the lifeline that delivered oxygen and food during pregnancy, has been cut. From now on, the baby will be dependent on its parents for protection, warmth, and food.

WEEK 14

Now roughly half the size of a banana, covered with fine hairs (lanugo), and starting to move around, the foetus has recognizable facial features. Its trunk has grown more in proportion than the legs with obvious quickly to be more developed than arms and wrists. fingers

WEEK 20

At the halfway mark of pregnancy, the fetus is around 6.7 in (17 cm) long, is developing the skin ridges that produce fingerprints, and fills its mother's expanding uterus. Kicking movements are felt by the mother, and the fetus' brain is developing rapidly. The fetus now follows phases of sleeping and waking, and can swallow and blink.

WEEK 40 FULL TERM

Between 38 and 40 weeks after fertilization, the fetus is around 21.7 in (55 cm) long, and ready developed. The fetus is equipped with survival in the to be born. The reflex, that will help circulating antibodies to be sucking reflex, that will help with survival in the as will the disease-fighting hormones into the outside world. blood. Now, the mother's push the foetus into the of the uterus to push the foetus.

37

INHERITANCE

We are what we are largely because of the genes we inherit from our parents. A mother's egg and a father's sperm both carry one set of their chromosomes—structures made of DNA that store genes. At fertilization, sperm and egg fuse to create the full complement of chromosomes needed to build a new human being. The child inherits from its parents a new combination of genes that will make it resemble them, but also make the new child unique.

CHROMOSOMES ▼

Inside the nucleus of every body cell there are 46 chromosomes, grouped into 23 pairs. Each chromosome is made of a long strand of DNA. When a cell is about to divide, the usually long and stringy chromosomes take on an X-shape, as shown here. In each pair of chromosomes, one comes from the mother and one from the father. Each pair carries the same genes at the same positions.

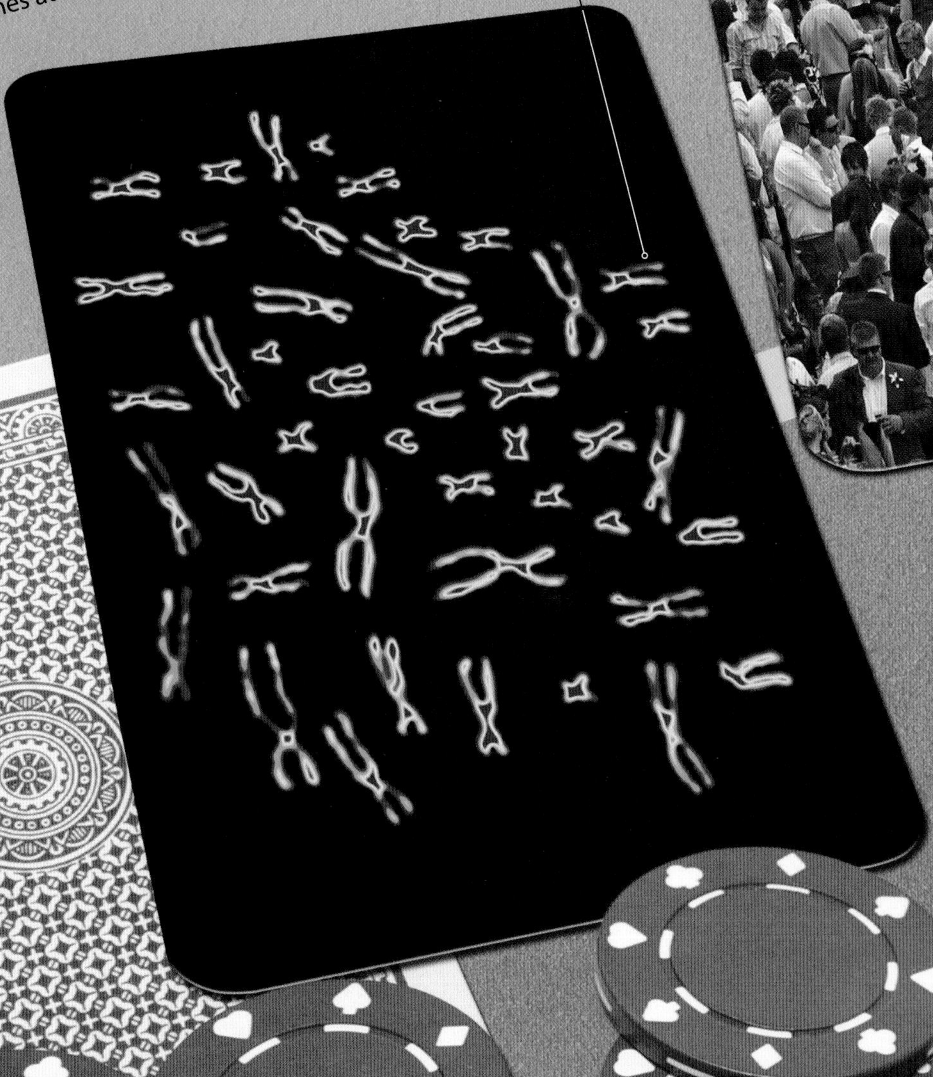

Each chromosome contains many genes

▲ SHARING DNA

You might think that this group of people appears very diverse, but any two of these people will share 99.9 percent of their DNA. When it comes to family members, that goes up to 99.95 percent. That explains why we all look basically the same, but with small differences that give us individuality.

◀ FAMILIES

It is often quite easy to recognize members of the same family because of similarities between them, but there are also differences. Children inherit one set of gene instructions from their mother and one from their father. Each child, therefore, has a unique gene combination that gives it a resemblance to its mother and father, but also unique features of its own.

▶ TWINS

Mothers usually have one baby at a time, but around one in every 60 births produces twins. Some twins, like these girls, are identical. They share exactly the same genes because, just after fertilization, the fertilized egg splits into two separate, identical cells. Most twins, though, are non-identical, the result of two eggs being fertilized at the same time. They are no more alike than other brothers and sisters.

◀ DOMINANT OR RECESSIVE

The genes a child inherits from his parents may come in different versions, called alleles, that can be dominant or recessive. If a dominant allele, such as the one that causes tongue rolling, is inherited from one or both parents, the child will be able to roll their tongue. A recessive allele, such as the one that makes tongue rolling impossible, has to be received from both parents.

QUICK THINKING
Brain cells relay the high-speed messages that control all our actions. These include directing the muscles that move our skeleton, and giving us sensations of the world around us.

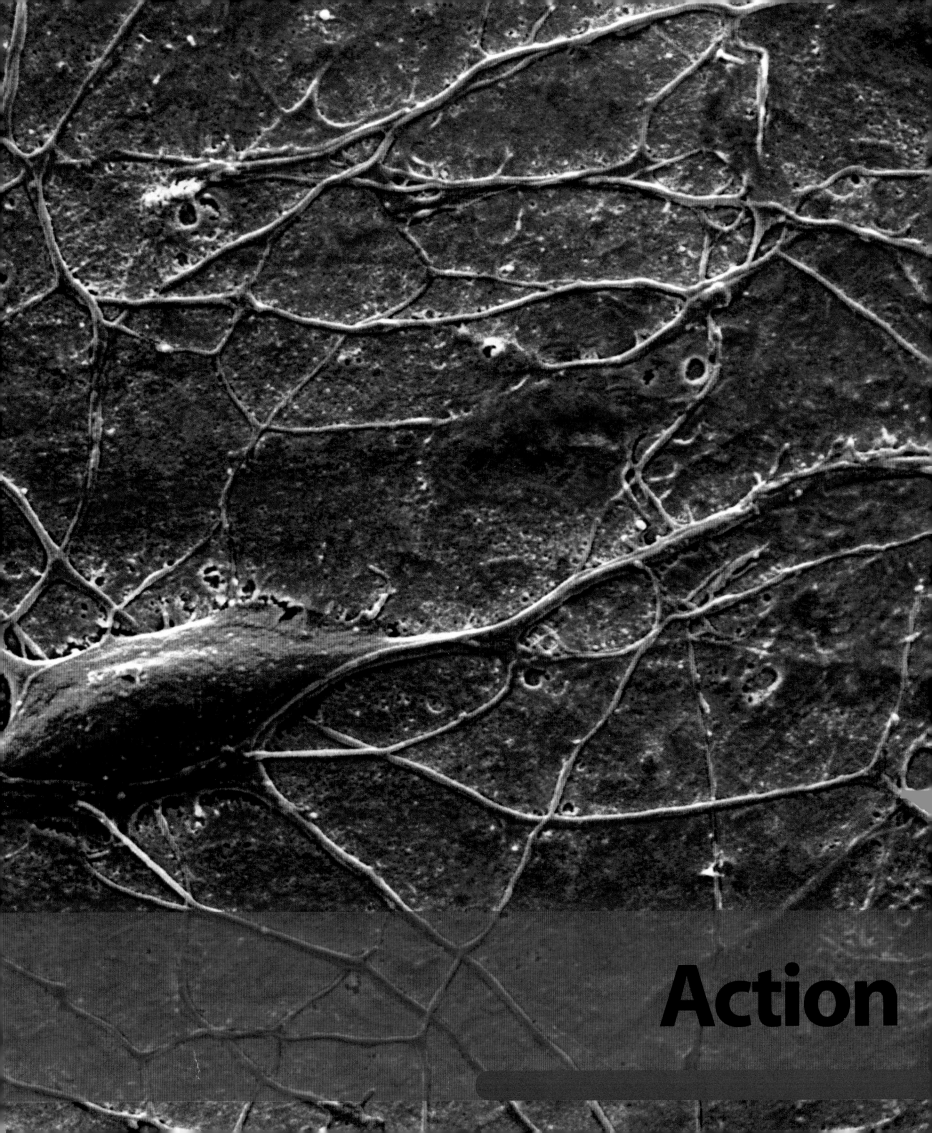

Action

FRAMEWORK

Without its bony framework, your body would collapse in a heap. Not only does your skeleton support and shape you, but it also protects vital organs such as the heart and brain. Moreover, your skeleton is flexible because of the movable joints between bones. Those bones anchor the muscles that create a vast array of movements. Some body parts, such as the nose and ears, are supported by flexible cartilage.

▼ BACKBONE

A tower of 26 odd-shaped bones called vertebrae make up the backbone. Vertebrae are separated by disks of cartilage, each with a tough coat and a squashy center. Disks allow limited movement between pairs of vertebrae. Together, however, they give the backbone considerable flexibility, so that the body can twist and turn, and bend from side to side and back and forth. The disks also act as shock absorbers when you walk, run, or jump.

► SKELETON

Making around 20 percent of the body's weight, an adult skeleton is constructed from 206 bones. The core supporting part of the skeleton, known as the axial skeleton, consists of the 80 bones that make up the backbone and its attachments—the skull, ribs, and sternum. The remaining 126 bones make up the appendicular skeleton—the arms and legs, and the girdles that link them to the axial skeleton. The thigh bones or femurs, for example, are attached by the strong pelvic girdle.

Skull
Lower jaw
Cervical vertebrae
Sternum
Rib
Lumbar vertebrae
Humerus
Radius
Ulna
Pelvic girdle
Carpals
Metacarpals
Phalanges
Femur

EAR FLAP ▼

The shell-shaped ear flap directs sound waves into the inner part of the ear, where hearing happens. It is supported by elastic cartilage, which combines strength with stretchability. If you pull your ear flap forward and then let go, it immediately springs back into place. Elastic cartilage also supports the epiglottis, the flap in your throat that stops food going down the wrong way during swallowing.

► NOSE SUPPORT

Your nose is supported by both bone and cartilage. While the bridge of the nose is shaped by skull bones, a framework of hyaline cartilage gives the end of the nose its bendiness. Both firm and flexible, hyaline cartilage is the most common type of cartilage. It also covers the ends of bones in joints, connects the ribs to the sternum, and forms the skeleton in developing babies.

Tibia

Fibula

Tarsals

Metatarsals

▶ DEVELOPING SKELETON

The skeleton starts to develop very early in a baby's life inside its mother. The first "bones", made of cartilage, form the template for the skeleton. Then, a process called ossification gradually replaces cartilage with bone. In this 14-week-old fetus, you can see bone (red), while cartilage remains colorless. Ossification continues as the skeleton grows, and is completed by the late teens.

▼ FEMALE AND MALE PELVIS

As well as attaching the thigh bones, the bowl-shaped pelvis supports and protects organs in the lower abdomen. It consists of two pelvic or hipbones that together form the pelvic girdle, and the sacrum, part of the backbone. The pelvis differs between males and females. In particular, its central opening is wider in females to provide enough room for a baby's head to pass through during birth.

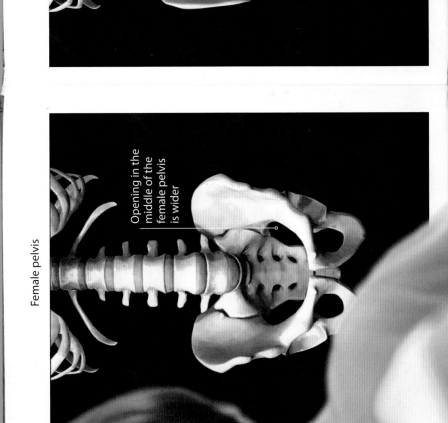

Male pelvis

Narrower pelvis supports male's stronger muscles

Female pelvis

Opening in the middle of the female pelvis is wider

BONES

These living organs consist of a matrix of collagen fibers, which produce strength and slight springiness, and mineral salts, particularly calcium phosphate, which give hardness. This matrix is made and maintained by bone cells. Bones are both strong and light because denser, heavier bone tissue is found only on their outsides, with lighter, spongy bone inside. As well as supporting the body, bones also make blood cells and store calcium.

❶ BONE STRUCTURE

This cutaway view of a long bone, such as the humerus, reveals its structure. Long bones have a shaft (diaphysis) and two broader ends (epiphyses) that form joints with other bones. Beneath an outer layer of compact bone is a layer of lighter, spongy bone. A central cavity is filled with bone marrow, while the bone is covered by a membrane (periosteum).

❷ COMPACT BONE

Dense, compact bone is constructed from weight-bearing "pillar" units called osteons—shown here as if sliced through the middle—that run in parallel along the length of a bone. Each osteon consists of concentric tubes of matrix, a structure that makes it really hard and strong. A central canal carries blood vessels that supply bone cells.

❸ OSTEOCYTES

These spiky bone cells are located in individual spaces in the bone matrix. They help to keep the bone in good shape. Osteocytes communicate with each other, and with the bone's blood supply, through tiny processes that pass along narrow canals. This allows the cells to obtain food and oxygen, and to get rid of waste.

Blood vessels

Spongy bone

Compact bone

Weight-bearing struts are separated by a maze of spaces

❹ SPONGY BONE

Also called cancellous bone, spongy bone is found beneath the layer of compact bone. It consists of a network of bony struts, and the spaces between the struts are usually filled with bone marrow. This honeycomb structure makes spongy bone much lighter than compact bone, but it is still very strong.

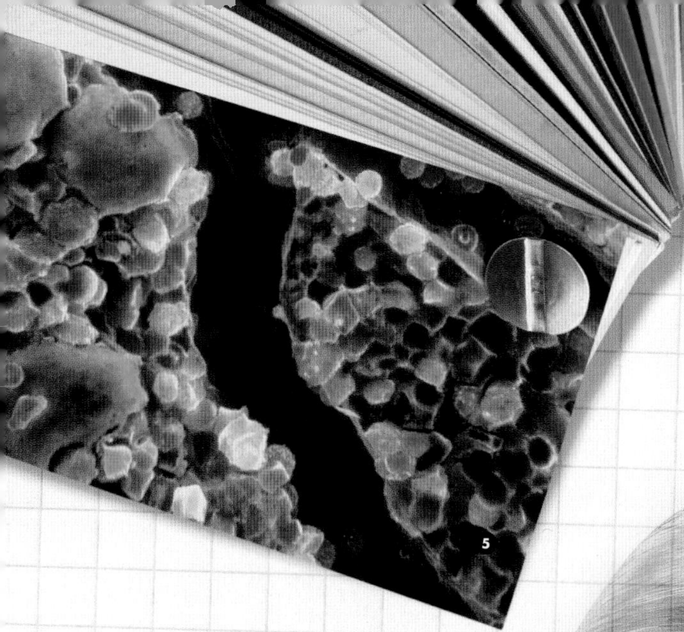

❺ BONE MARROW

This is red bone marrow, a soft tissue found mainly inside flat bones, such as the shoulder blades and ribs. It produces billions of red and white blood cells (shown in red and blue) daily to replace those that have worn out. Yellow bone marrow, found mainly in the central cavity of long bones, stores fat.

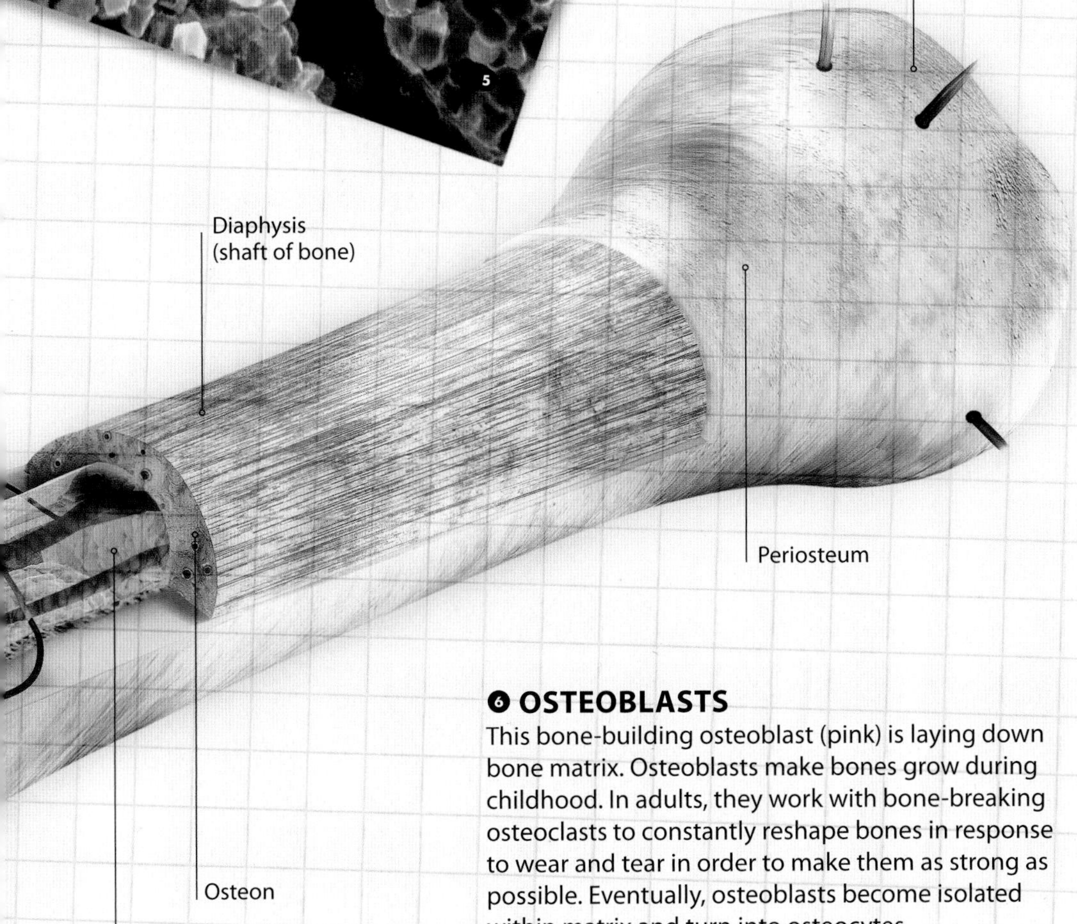

Epiphysis (expanded head of bone)

Diaphysis (shaft of bone)

Periosteum

Osteon

Bone marrow

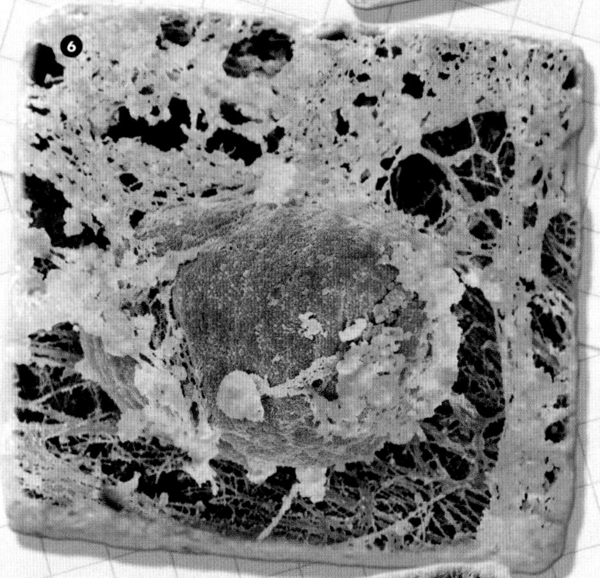

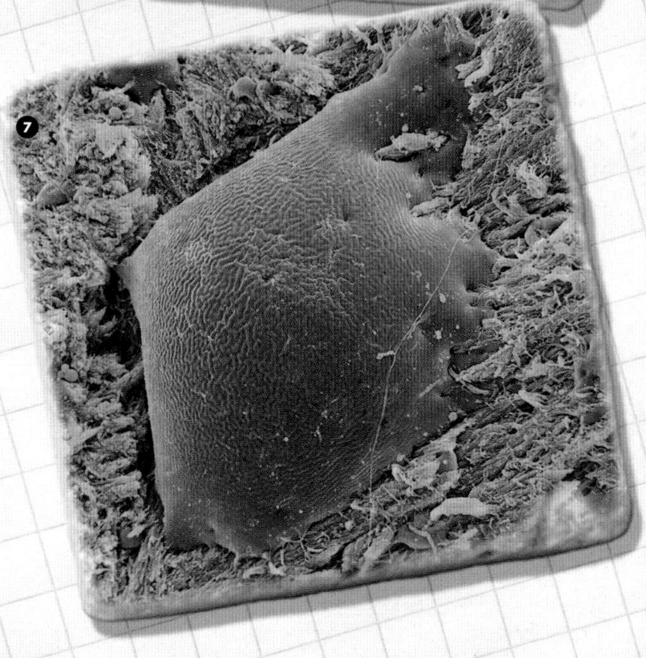

❻ OSTEOBLASTS

This bone-building osteoblast (pink) is laying down bone matrix. Osteoblasts make bones grow during childhood. In adults, they work with bone-breaking osteoclasts to constantly reshape bones in response to wear and tear in order to make them as strong as possible. Eventually, osteoblasts become isolated within matrix and turn into osteocytes.

❼ OSTEOCLASTS

These giant cells (pink) have the opposite effect to osteoblasts. They break down bone matrix by digging away at its surface. As osteoclasts work, they release calcium—essential for normal nerve and muscle action—into the blood, while osteoblasts return it to store in bone matrix. This balancing act serves to control calcium levels in the blood.

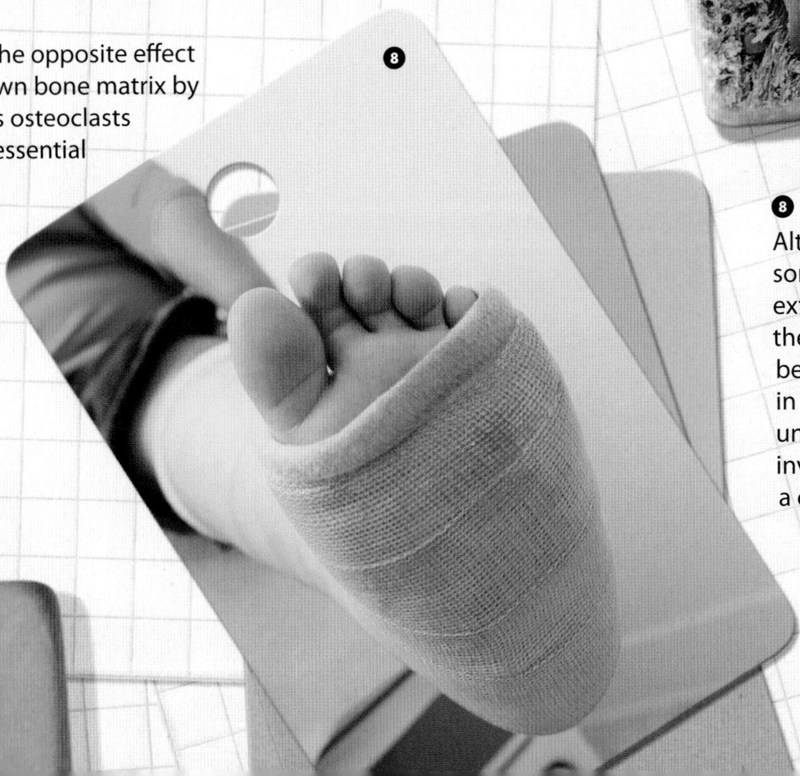

❽ BROKEN BONES

Although bones are strong, they sometimes break or fracture if put under extreme pressure. Broken bones repair themselves, but the bone ends need to be lined up to ensure they stay together in the right position and do not move until healing is completed. This may involve immobilizing a body part with a cast, as shown here. Alternatively, pins or plates may be used to hold bones together.

▼ CRANIAL BONES

Eight cranial bones construct the cranium, the thin but remarkably strong domed part of the skull that supports and surrounds the brain. The frontal bone forms the cranium's front, the two parietal bones its side and roof, the two temporal bones the sides, the occipital bone its rear and base, the sphenoid part of its floor, and the ethmoid bone part of the nasal cavity.

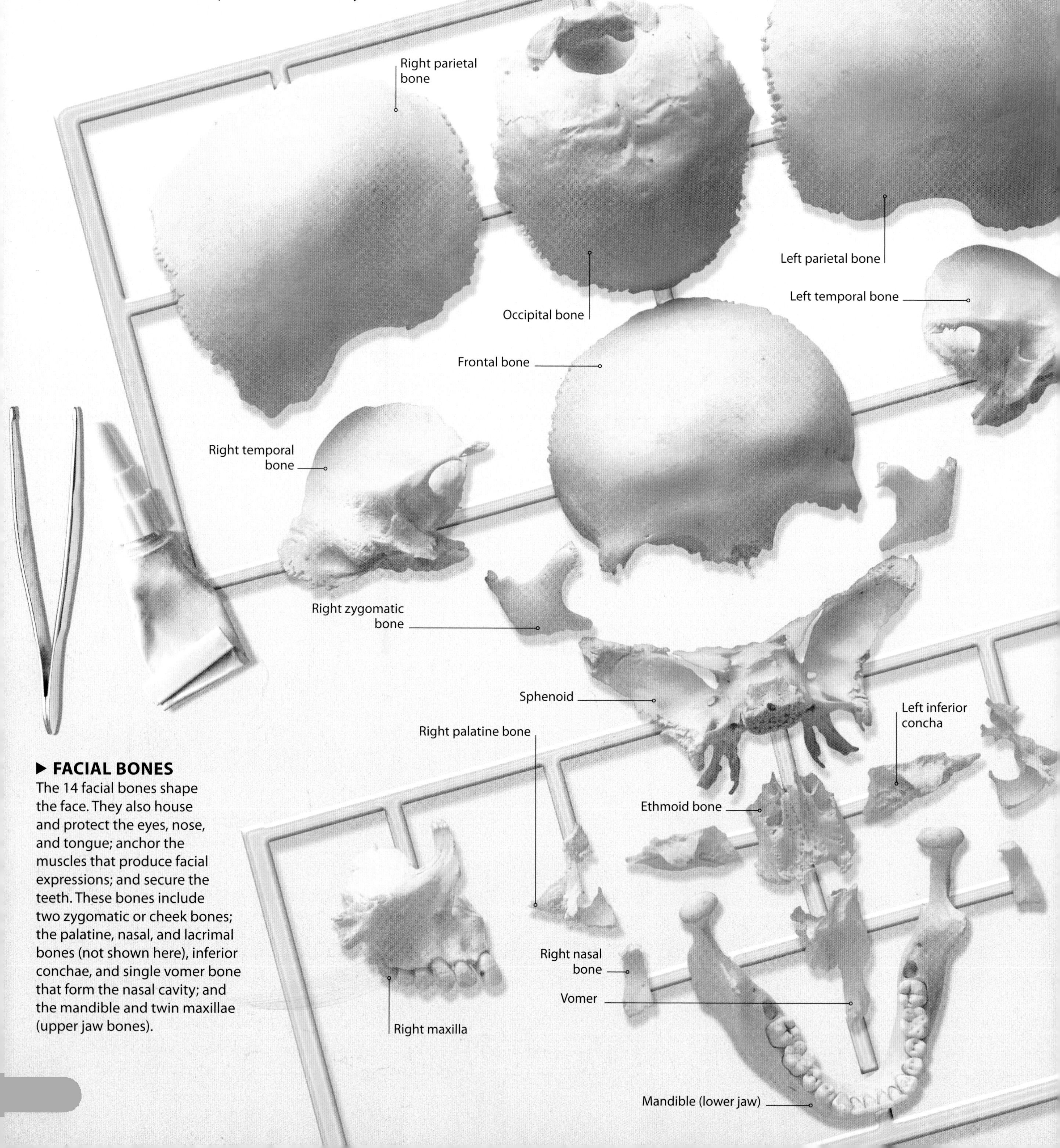

Right parietal bone

Left parietal bone

Left temporal bone

Occipital bone

Frontal bone

Right temporal bone

Right zygomatic bone

Sphenoid

Left inferior concha

Right palatine bone

▶ FACIAL BONES

The 14 facial bones shape the face. They also house and protect the eyes, nose, and tongue; anchor the muscles that produce facial expressions; and secure the teeth. These bones include two zygomatic or cheek bones; the palatine, nasal, and lacrimal bones (not shown here), inferior conchae, and single vomer bone that form the nasal cavity; and the mandible and twin maxillae (upper jaw bones).

Ethmoid bone

Right nasal bone

Vomer

Right maxilla

Mandible (lower jaw)

SKULL

The most complex part of our skeleton is undoubtedly the skull. It is constructed from not one but 22 bones, most of which are locked together to make the skull incredibly strong. Those normally interlocked bones can be seen separately in the "exploded" view of the skull on the facing page. Such strength is essential in order to protect the delicate brain along with the ears and eyes. The skull also shapes our head and face.

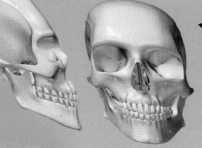

◀ LIGHT BUT STRONG
The skull is basically a bony sphere with face-supporting bones at the front and brain-protecting bones making up the rest of it. Many of the skull's bones are thin and flattened, helping to make it light without losing strength. The skull's weight is further reduced by air-filled cavities, called sinuses, inside certain skull bones. Other cavities house the ears, eyes, and nose.

▶ SKULL HOLES
This view of the base of the skull shows the foramen magnum, the opening through which the spinal cord passes from the base of the brain. This is by far the biggest of the foramina (the plural of "foramen"), or holes that pierce the skull. Through these foramina pass blood vessels that serve the brain along with cranial nerves that sprout from the brain.

Foramen magnum

◀ SUTURES
Apart from the lower jaw, all skull bones are locked together by immovable joints called sutures. The bones' jagged edges fit together like pieces in a jigsaw puzzle. In younger people, a layer of fibrous tissue binds sutures together, but still allows bones to grow at their edges so the skull can expand. By middle age, the skull bones have fused together completely.

▶ OPEN AND CLOSE
Although 21 of the skull's 22 bones are locked together, the mandible or lower jaw forms movable joints with the temporal bones, enabling it to open and close. That's fortunate because it allows us to breathe, speak, sing, yawn, bite, chew, and drink. The U-shaped mandible is the biggest and strongest facial bone. It also contains sockets in which 16 teeth are embedded.

Sagittal suture between left and right parietal bones

JOINTS

The human body can perform an incredible range of movements. That is only possible because the skeleton has joints located wherever two or more bones meet. Most of the body's 400 joints are free-moving synovial joints that provide both flexibility and, by holding bones together, stability. A few joints, such as those between skull bones, are fixed, while others, like those in the backbone, allow limited movements.

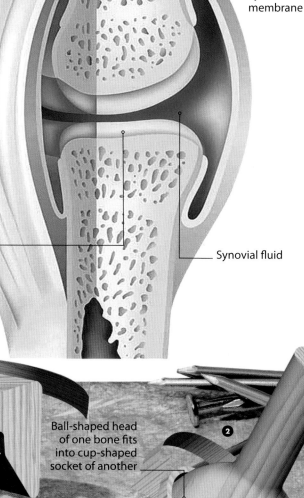

Bone marrow

Bone

Ligaments

Joint capsule

Synovial membrane

Hyaline cartilage

Synovial fluid

▶ SYNOVIAL JOINTS

Inside a typical synovial joint, each bone end is capped with, and protected by, glassy hyaline cartilage. Oily synovial fluid, which fills the space between the two bones, makes the cartilages really slippery, so the joint moves smoothly with hardly any friction. Synovial fluid is made by a synovial membrane that lines the joint capsule. The capsule holds the joint together and is often reinforced by straplike ligaments.

▶ TYPES OF JOINT

There are six basic types of synovial joint in your body— pivot, ball-and-socket, hinge, plane, ellipsoidal, and saddle. They differ according to how the bone ends fit together. This controls the range of movements allowed by each joint type, as does how tightly the bone ends are held together by ligaments. For example, the hinge joint in the elbow allows the forearm to move back and forth, like a door opening or closing. The ball-and-socket joint in the shoulder permits movement in most directions.

Projection from one bone turns within hollow in another bone

❶

Ball-shaped head of one bone fits into cup-shaped socket of another

❷

❶ **Pivot joint** You can shake your head to say "No" because of a pivot joint. The backbone's topmost vertebra swivels around a bony projection from the second vertebra to allow the head to turn. A pivot joint in the elbow lets the forearm rotate.

❷ **Ball-and-socket joint** This is the most flexible type of joint in the body. Found in the shoulder, between the humerus and shoulder blade, and in the hip, between the femur and pelvic girdle, the ball-and-socket joint allows rotation in most directions.

▼ DISLOCATED JOINTS

This X ray shows a dislocated joint in the little finger. Dislocation happens when a sudden wrench or blow forces bones out of line. It happens most commonly in finger joints, as here, and the shoulder joint. The joint capsule holding the bones together can be damaged by dislocation, causing pain and swelling. Doctors treat dislocated joints by moving bones back into their correct positions.

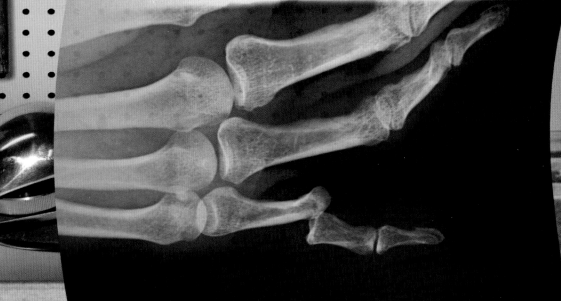

❸ **Hinge joint** Found in the knee and elbow, and between finger and toe bones, hinge joints, as their name suggests, work like a door hinge to allow movement in just one direction. This enables a body part, such as the arm, to bend or straighten.

❹ **Plane joint** While most joints either rotate or hinge against each other, plane joints allow limited gliding movements from side to side. With their flat bone ends being held tightly together, they give limited flexibility to wrist and ankle bones.

❺ **Ellipsoidal joint** Sometimes called a condyloid joint, the ellipsoidal joint allows bones to move from side to side or backwards and forwards. These joints are found at the base of fingers and toes, and in the wrist.

Bone endings fit together like a horse rider on a saddle

❻

Curved end of one bone turns in cylindrical ending of another

❸

❹

❺

Flat endings of bones slide over each other

❻ **Saddle joint** Consisting of two U-shaped surfaces set at right angles, the saddle joint is located at the base of the thumb. It gives the thumb considerable mobility, allowing it to sweep across the palm and touch all of the fingertips.

Oval ending of one bone moves in a cavity in the other bone's ending

49

MUSCLES

Without muscles, we would be unable to move. The cells, known as fibers, that make up muscles have the unique ability to contract and create a pulling force. There are three distinct types of muscles in the body—skeletal, smooth, and cardiac. Some 640 skeletal muscles, which help shape the body and make up some 40 percent of its mass, move and support the skeleton. Smooth muscle tissue is found in the walls of hollow organs such as the stomach. Cardiac muscle tissue produces the pumping action of the heart.

❶ NAMING MUSCLES

The Latin names given to skeletal muscles may seem complex, but they simply reflect features, such as the action, shape, size, or attachments of muscles. For example, extensors, such as the extensor digitorum, straighten joints. The deltoid (triangular) and trapezius (four-sided) are named for their shapes. The gluteus maximus—"maximus" means big—is the body's bulkiest muscle. And the biceps brachii—"biceps" means two heads—has two attachments connecting it through tendons to the shoulder blade.

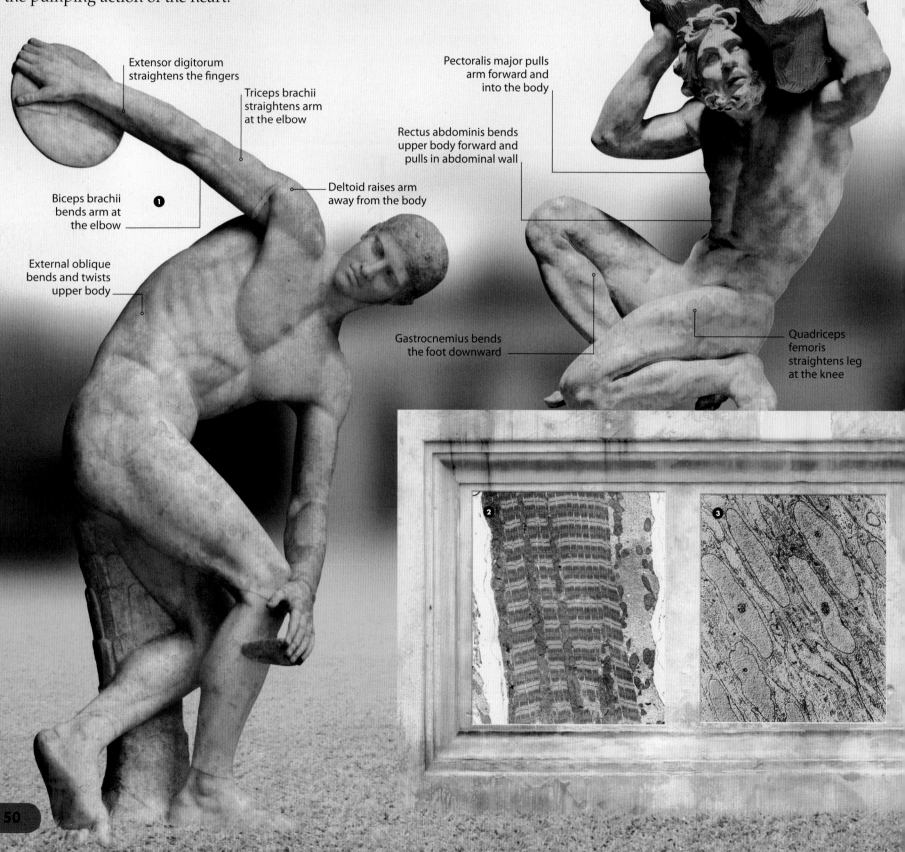

Extensor digitorum straightens the fingers

Triceps brachii straightens arm at the elbow

Biceps brachii bends arm at the elbow ❶

Deltoid raises arm away from the body

External oblique bends and twists upper body

Pectoralis major pulls arm forward and into the body

Rectus abdominis bends upper body forward and pulls in abdominal wall

Gastrocnemius bends the foot downward

Quadriceps femoris straightens leg at the knee

❷ SKELETAL MUSCLES

Also called voluntary muscles because you decide to move them, skeletal muscles pull bones. Under the microscope, the fibers that make up skeletal muscles appear stripy. That's because they are packed with rodlike, striped myofibrils that are lined up to give an overall stripy effect. More importantly, they contain the mechanism that makes skeletal muscles contract.

❸ SMOOTH MUSCLES

Among many other things, smooth muscles push food along your intestines and squeeze urine out of your bladder. Smooth muscles are found particularly in the walls of hollow organs and are controlled, without you being aware, by the body's autopilot—the autonomic nervous system—and by hormones. Smooth muscles have short fibers with tapering ends. These fibers (pink) with large nuclei (yellow) from the uterus wall push out the baby during birth.

❹ CARDIAC MUSCLES

Found solely in the heart, cardiac muscles contract automatically and tirelessly to pump blood. The fibers branch to form an interconnected network. Each fiber contains masses of big mitochondria (brown) that provide the energy needed to keep it contracting without a break. Between the mitochondria are myofibrils (green), which contain the filaments that interact to cause contraction.

❺

Trapezius pulls head and shoulders backward

Latissimus dorsi pulls arm downward, backward, and inward

Gluteus maximus pulls the thigh backward

Erector spinae straightens the back

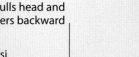
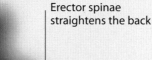

❹

"Hamstring" bends leg at the knee

❺ BODY BUILDING

A female bodybuilder shows off her clearly defined muscles. Bodybuilders develop their physique through exercise and diet. They take exercise to extremes in order to cause the fibers in their skeletal muscles to expand so that their muscles become massively enlarged. They use a special diet that's high in protein to reduce their body fat so that their muscles stand out even more clearly.

MOVEMENT

These gym members are using their skeletal muscles to move their bodies. Muscles do this by contracting, or getting shorter, to pull the bones of the skeleton across joints. They contract when instructed to do so by signals from the brain and spinal cord. These signals trigger changes inside the muscle that convert stored energy to movement energy, creating a pulling power that is sufficient to produce movement.

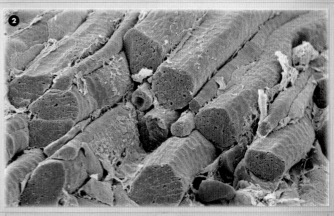

❶ MUSCLE STRUCTURE

Skeletal muscles have a highly ordered structure, as shown in this exploded view. A muscle is made up of bundles of long muscle fibers (cells). Each fiber is packed with rodlike myofibrils that contain arrays of overlapping thick and thin protein filaments. When a muscle contracts, the filaments interact, using energy to slide over each other to make it shorter.

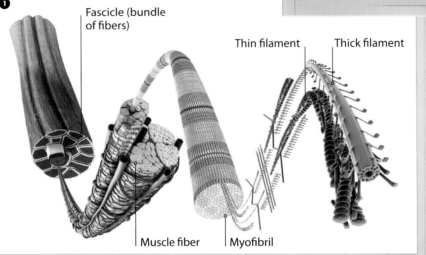

Fascicle (bundle of fibers)

Thin filament

Thick filament

Muscle fiber

Myofibril

❷ MUSCLE FIBERS

The fibers that make up skeletal muscles are well adapted to the job they do. Shown here in cross section, skeletal muscle fibers are cylindrical, can reach up to 12 in (30 cm) long, and run parallel to each other along a muscle. When muscle fibers contract together, they can generate the great pulling power needed to move bones.

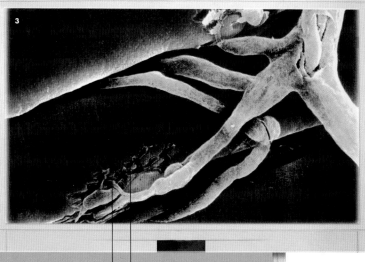

Muscle fiber | Motor neuron terminal

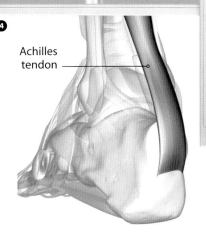

Achilles tendon

Biceps relaxes

Triceps contracts

Biceps contracts

Triceps relaxes

❸ NERVE-MUSCLE JUNCTION

Skeletal muscles are also called voluntary muscles because we, via the nervous system, decide to make them contract. Nerves and muscles make contact at nerve-muscle junctions. Motor neurons, which carry instructions from the brain and spinal cord, branch into terminals (green) that each form a nerve-muscle junction with a muscle fiber (red). It is here that nerve impulses pass into the muscle fiber and make it contract.

❹ TENDONS

These tough cords connect skeletal muscles to bones. When muscles contract, tendons pull bones so that they move at joints. Tendons are packed with parallel bundles of strong collagen fibers that give them tremendous tensile (pulling) strength. The body's biggest tendon is the Achilles, or calcaneal, tendon in the heel. It links the calf muscles, which bend the foot downward, to the heel bone.

❺ ANTAGONISTIC MUSCLES

Muscles perform work by contracting and pulling. When they relax and lengthen, they do so passively. As a consequence, moving a body part in two directions requires muscles with opposite, or antagonistic, actions. In the arm, for example, the triceps brachii muscle in the back of the upper arm contracts to straighten the elbow, while the biceps brachii muscle contracts to bend the elbow.

The fingers and thumb on each hand are made up of 14 bones, called phalanges—two in the thumb, and three in each finger. There are 14 joints, known as knuckles, in the fingers: nine hinge joints between the phalanges themselves, and five more freely moving ellipsoidal joints between the phalanges and the metacarpals, or palm bones. Together, these joints give the hand the flexibility needed to perform its many tasks.

HANDS

Our hands can perform a vast range of different roles, from those that are very powerful, such as lifting objects, to those that are extremely precise, such as painting. Such versatility is possible because the many bones that make up the hand create a flexible framework that is moved by more than 30 muscles. Most of these muscles are in the forearm, attached to the hand bones by long tendons.

Fingers curl round to grasp objects

Cloth held between thumb and fingers

Index finger can be extended for pointing

▲ DIFFERENT ACTIONS

Thanks to the flexibility of its bony framework, the opposability of the thumb, and the many muscles controlling its movements, the human hand can perform lots of different actions. These range from the strength of a power grip, produced when the fingers and thumb are clasped tightly around an object, to a much more delicate precision grip such as threading a needle or holding a pen.

Tendons from muscles
in the forearm pass
through the wrist

Extensor retinaculum
wraps around wrist to
hold tendons in place

▶ FRONT MUSCLES

Long tendons extend from muscles in the front of the forearm. Most of these muscles are flexors that bend either the wrist or the fingers or thumb. The flexor digitorum superficialis, for example, bends the fingers so they can grip. Muscles within the hand itself make its movements more precise.

▶ BACK MUSCLES

Muscles in the back of the forearm are mostly extensors that either straighten the wrist or the fingers or thumb. For example, the extensor digitorum pulls on the fingers to straighten them. The long tendons of these muscles, and those found in the front of the arm, are held in place, and prevented from bulging outward, by a fibrous "wristband" called a retinaculum. Smaller muscles working inside the hand include the dorsal interosseus that spreads the fingers.

Flexor digiti minimi bends little finger

Abductor pollicis brevis pulls thumb out to the side

Tendon of extensor digitorum

Dorsal interosseus

Tendon of flexor digitorum superficialis

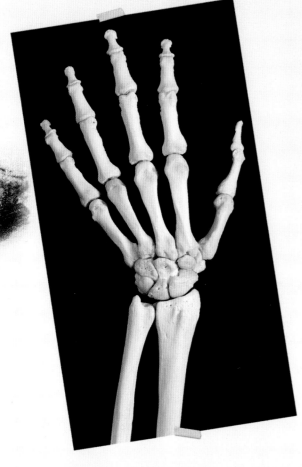

OPPOSABLE THUMB ▼

A key feature of the hand is its opposable thumb. Being opposable means that it can swing across the palm and bend and turn toward the fingers in such a way that its tip can touch the other fingers. This action, called opposition, enables the hand to grasp and pick up small objects. Opposition also creates the precision grip needed to, for example, hold a paint brush.

▲ HAND BONES

The 27 bones in each hand are divided into three groups—carpals, metacarpals, and phalanges. There are eight carpals in the wrist, and these allow limited movement and give the hand stability. The palm of the hand is made up of five long, straight metacarpals, and 14 phalanges form the fingers or digits.

EXERCISE

Every day, our bodies experience different levels of activity from sitting in a chair to running up a flight of stairs. Obviously, running requires our muscles to work harder than sitting. The body adjusts automatically to changes in activity. How well it makes these adjustments depends on its fitness—the ability to perform an action without getting breathless or exhausted. Fitness is made up of three elements—strength, stamina, and flexibility—and all three can be improved by regular exercise.

▼ STRENGTH

The amount of force that your muscles can exert when, for example, you lift an object, is determined by their strength. One of the best ways to improve muscle strength is through repetitive resistance exercises such as lifting weights. Over time such exercises increase the size, and therefore the pulling power, of muscle fibers. Brief and intensive, these exercises require quick bursts of energy supplied by anaerobic respiration, which does not need oxygen.

▼ STAMINA

Also called cardiovascular fitness or endurance, stamina is a measure of how efficiently the heart and skeletal muscles work. During aerobic exercise, such as fast walking, running, or swimming, muscles generate energy using aerobic respiration, which requires oxygen to "burn" fuels such as glucose. Taking aerobic exercise regularly, at least three times a week, significantly improves stamina by making the heart stronger, so it can deliver oxygen and fuel more efficiently, and by increasing the blood supply to the muscles.

69

▶ BENEFITS

Regular exercise, especially aerobic exercise, makes us feel happier and more alert. It also helps us keep our weight at the right level and remove excess fat. It can increase muscle mass and can increase muscle mass and remove excess fat. As this chart shows, each type of exercise has different benefits in terms of improving strength, stamina, or flexibility. Swimming, for example, is a really good exercise because it increases all three aspects of fitness.

BENEFITS OF DIFFERENT EXERCISES

ACTIVITY	STRENGTH	STAMINA	FLEXIBILITY
Swimming	★★★	★★★★	★★★★
Walking briskly	★	★★★★	★★
Running	★★	★★★★★	★★
Cycling fast	★★	★★★★★	★★★
Dancing	★★	★★★	★★★★
Yoga	★	★	★★★★
Basketball	★★	★★★	★★
Tennis	★★	★★★	★★★
Climbing stairs	★★★	★★★	★

▶ FLEXIBILITY

How easily you can bend and straighten your body shows how flexible you are. Flexibility depends on the ability of joints, aided by tendons and ligaments, to move freely. Exercises that improve flexibility include yoga, gymnastics, and dance. These all involve stretching and holding, ensuring that joints stay in good condition and that muscles are as supple as possible.

Tendons and ligaments allow joints to move freely

Sweat glands are found all over the body, except the palms and soles

▶ EFFECTS OF EXERCISE

Whenever you exercise, your body's internal activities change, in particular to deliver more oxygen and fuel to your muscles. Your breathing rate increases to get more oxygen into the bloodstream, while the heart rate soars to pump more blood to skeletal muscles. As muscles work harder to move the body, they release lots of heat. Excess heat is released through the skin by sweating to prevent the body from overheating.

BODY LANGUAGE

Communication is vitally important for humans. As well as spoken language, we use body language to pass on a multitude of messages about our moods and intentions. Facial expressions convey six basic emotions—surprise, anger, disgust, happiness, fear, and sadness—and many more in between. The body's position, posture, and gestures also show what we feel, whether we want them to or not.

❶ SURPRISE

This is a response to something unexpected or unknown. The frontalis muscle raises the eyebrows, which become strongly arched, and the forehead wrinkles. The eyes open wide, to take in more visual information, and the jaw drops. We use a variation of the surprise expression, called the eyebrow flash, to acknowledge people without talking to them.

❷ ANGER

People usually get angry to confront a real or imagined threat. Muscles pull the eyebrows downward and produce wrinkles between them. Orbicularis oculi muscles make the eyes narrower to create a glaring expression, and the mouth opens wider to expose the teeth. The overall effect is to make the face bigger, distorted, and more scary.

❸ DISGUST

Maybe she smelled something bad or saw something unpleasant, but it's clear from this person's face that she is feeling disgust. The orbicularis oris muscle surrounding the mouth purses the lips, depressor anguli oris muscles pull the corners of the mouth downward, the eyes narrow, and the eyebrows come down.

❹ HAPPINESS

A broad smile is often the outward sign of happiness. Zygomaticus muscles pull the corners of the mouth upward. At the same time, the levator labii superioris muscles lift the top lip to expose the teeth. A real smile—as opposed to one that is faked—lifts the cheeks and causes wrinkles around the eyes.

❺ FEAR

This basic emotion is closely related to anger, but it causes us to shrink away from threats rather than to confront them. The frontalis muscle wrinkles the forehead as it lifts the eyebrows, and the eyes open wider. The lips are pulled taut and the lower lip is pulled downward by the depressor labii inferioris muscle. The face looks paler as blood drains from the skin and toward the muscles.

❻ FACIAL MUSCLES

Our facial expressions are generated by more than 30 small facial muscles. These are anchored at one end to the skull and to the skin of the face at the other end. Carefully controlled by signals from the brain, facial muscles work with great precision by tugging small areas of skin to express outwardly the way we feel inwardly. Some of the main facial muscles are shown here.

❼ POSTURE AND GESTURE

We are often unaware of how we use our bodies to communicate our feelings to other people. Our posture—whether, for example, we angle ourselves toward or away from other people—says a lot about how we feel about them, as does how close we stand or sit to them. Gestures are important too, indicating whether we are being defensive, dishonest, dominant, submissive, or taking an interest.

❽ SADNESS

It's clear to an outside observer when someone is feeling sad. The mouth is closed by the orbicularis oris muscle, and is turned down at the edges by the depressor anguli oris muscles. The eyebrows rise at their inner ends, while tears often well up in the eyes. A hand, or hands, supports the "heavy-feeling" head, and also helps to cover the face.

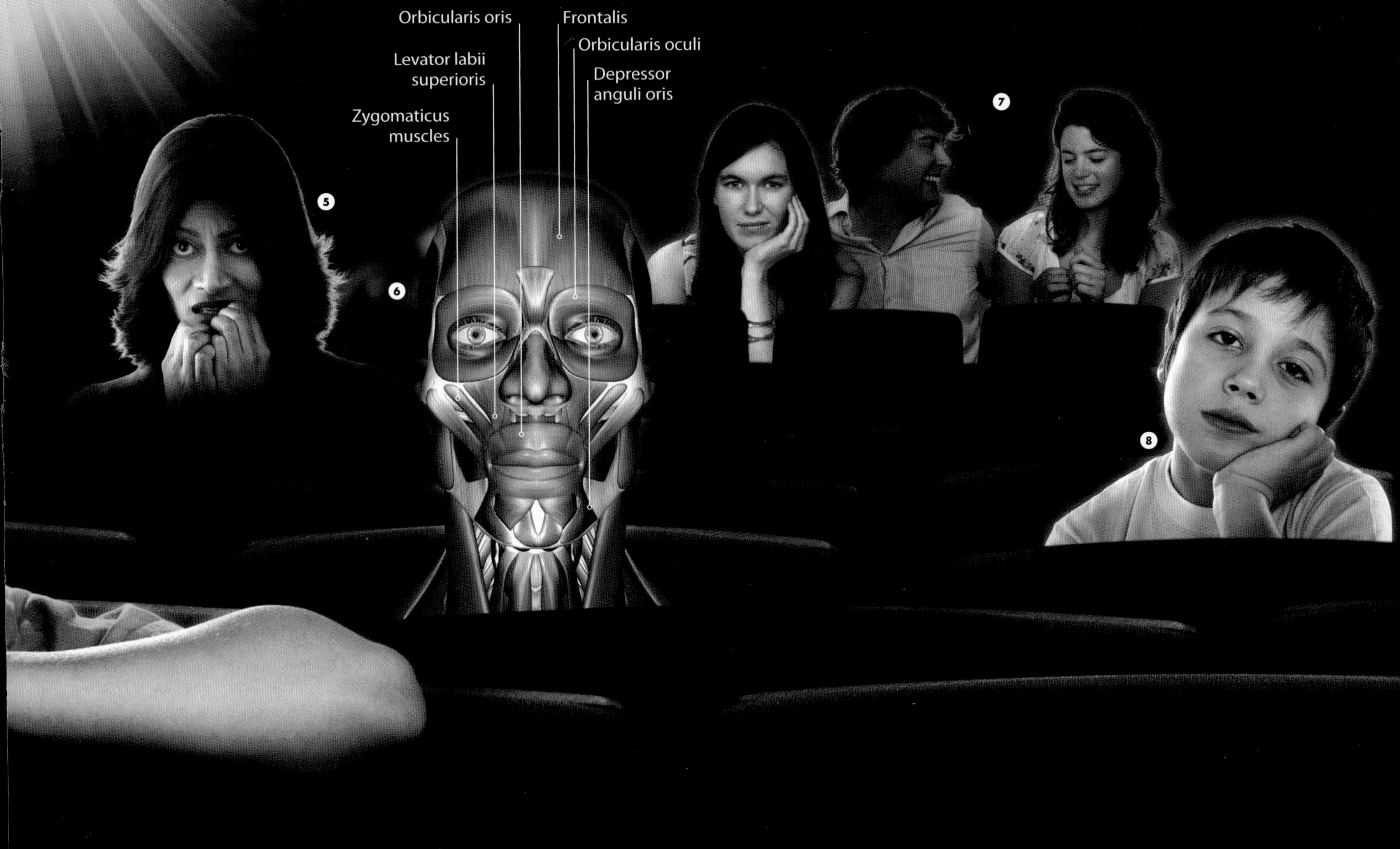

Orbicularis oris

Frontalis

Levator labii superioris

Orbicularis oculi

Zygomaticus muscles

Depressor anguli oris

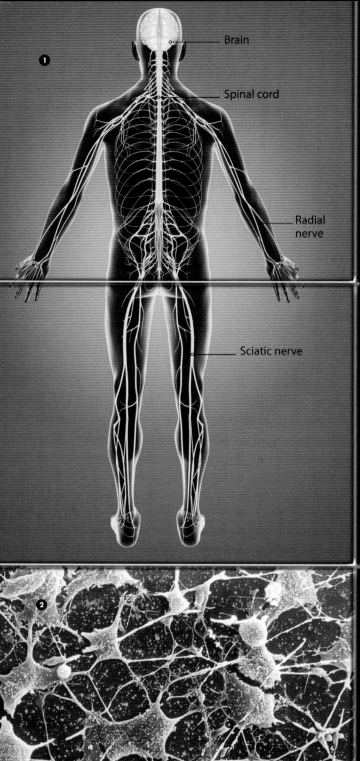

Brain

Spinal cord

Radial nerve

Sciatic nerve

IN CONTROL

All the activities that keep the body alive are constantly controlled by the nervous system. It works 24 hours a day, collecting information about how body parts are working, and sending out instructions accordingly to regulate those activities. The nervous system consists of a network of cells that generate, transmit, and interpret millions of electrical signals, giving it a processing power far greater than any computer, and the ability to deal with many tasks at once.

Cerebellum coordinates balance and movement

❶ NERVOUS SYSTEM

Your nervous system consists of two parts. The brain and spinal cord form the central nervous system, which is packed with nerve cells that receive and process information and send out instructions. Nerves are cablelike structures that form the peripheral nervous system. They are bundles of sensory and motor neurons that, respectively, carry messages to and from the spinal cord and brain.

Spinal cord extends from the base of the brain

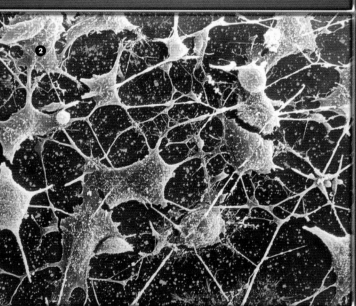

❷ NERVE CELLS

Neurons, or nerve cells, are building blocks that form the communication network of the nervous system. They carry tiny electrical signals, called impulses, that travel at high speed along slender processes or fibers that extend from central cell bodies (shown here). These fibers either pick up impulses from, or transmit them to, other neurons. Impulses "jump" from one neuron to another across gaps called synapses.

❸ CENTRAL NERVOUS SYSTEM

The brain and spinal cord make up your central nervous system or CNS. The job of the CNS is to control and coordinate all of your body's activities, from singing songs to digesting lunch. Your CNS is packed with neurons that receive and process input from sensory receptors, such as those in the eyes, and send out instructions to muscles and organs. They also store memories and let you imagine.

❹ SENSATION

You can read these words because of your nervous system. Sensory receptors in your eyes, ears, nose, tongue, skin, and elsewhere detect changes outside and inside your body. They send impulses along sensory neurons to update your CNS. Your brain processes these signals, so you can experience these sensations. Sensory messages from inside the body tell your brain, for example, when your bladder is full.

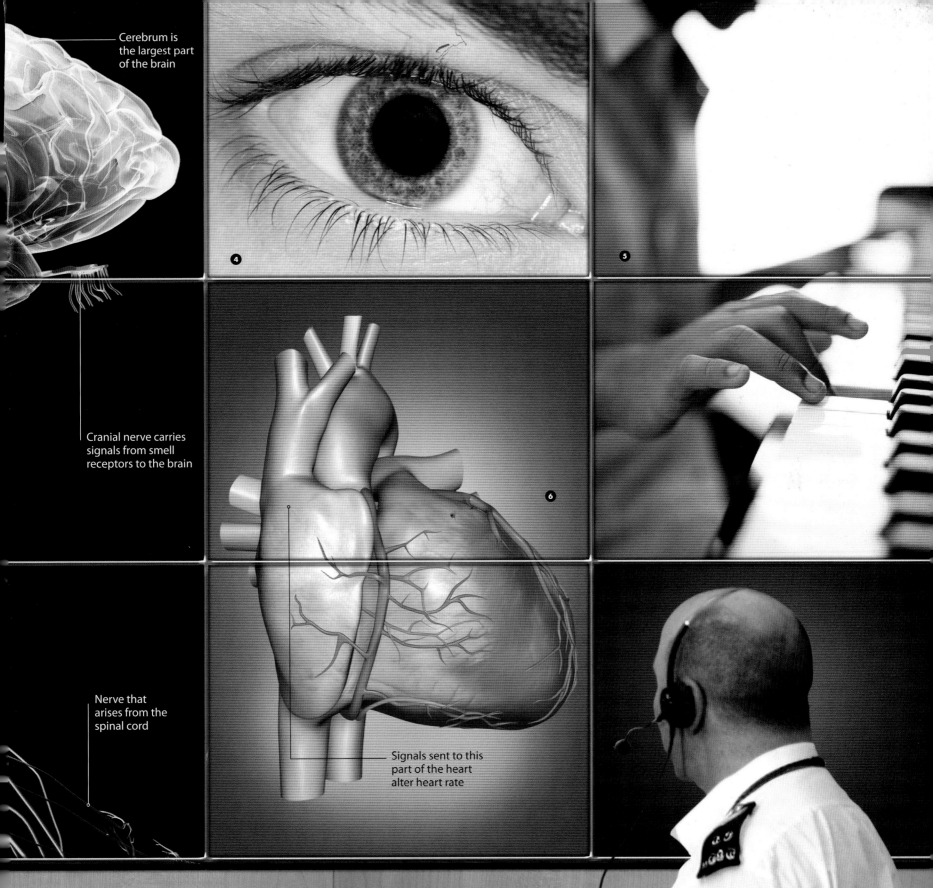

Cerebrum is the largest part of the brain

Cranial nerve carries signals from smell receptors to the brain

Nerve that arises from the spinal cord

Signals sent to this part of the heart alter heart rate

❺ MOVEMENT

Every movement you make, from playing the piano to jumping in the air, is controlled by your nervous system. Motor neurons carry instructions from the brain and spinal cord to the skeletal muscles that create movement. The cerebellum and parts of the cerebrum cooperate to ensure that signals to muscles are sent out with the right timing cend in the right sequence to produce smooth, coordinated movements.

❻ AUTONOMIC NERVOUS SYSTEM

Your autonomic nervous system (ANS) acts like an autopilot, automatically controlling all the activities going on inside your body without you being aware. This system of motor neurons carries signals from the brain that, for example, increase heart and breathing rates when you exercise. The ANS has two divisions with opposite actions that complement each other.

NEURONS

Found only in the nervous system, neurons, or nerve cells, have the unique ability to generate and transmit electrical signals called nerve impulses. All neurons are interconnected, so they create a vast communications network, the nervous system, that extends throughout the body. Neurons in the central nervous system (CNS)—the brain and spinal cord—process incoming information and issue instructions. Other neurons either transmit information from sensors to the CNS or carry signals to muscles telling them to contract.

❷ MOTOR NEURONS

These long neurons carry nerve impulses away from the CNS to effectors. The most important of these effectors include the muscles, which move the body in response to instructions from the brain, and glands such as the adrenal gland, which releases the hormone adrenaline when told to do so. The cell bodies of motor neurons are located in the spinal cord, where they receive messages from other neurons.

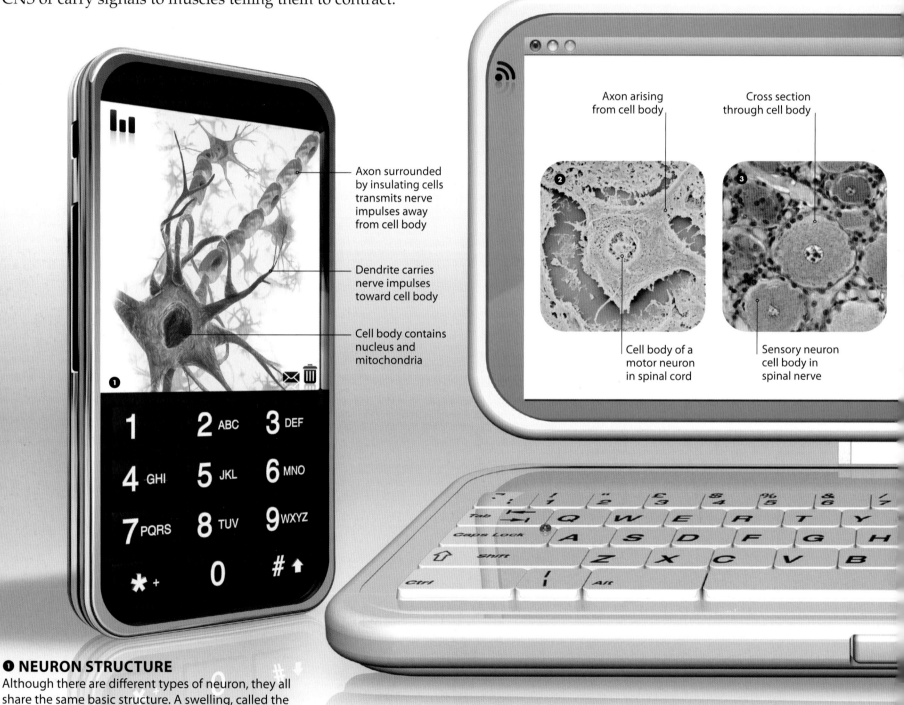

Axon surrounded by insulating cells transmits nerve impulses away from cell body

Dendrite carries nerve impulses toward cell body

Cell body contains nucleus and mitochondria

Axon arising from cell body

Cross section through cell body

Cell body of a motor neuron in spinal cord

Sensory neuron cell body in spinal nerve

❶ NEURON STRUCTURE

Although there are different types of neuron, they all share the same basic structure. A swelling, called the cell body, contains the nucleus and other structures usually found in a cell. Attached to the cell body are short filaments, called dendrites, that carry electrical signals, called nerve impulses, towards the cell body. A longer filament, called the axon or nerve fiber, carries nerve impulses away from the cell body.

❸ SENSORY NEURONS

As their name suggests, these long neurons carry sensory messages from the body to the CNS. Some sensory neurons are triggered directly by stimuli such as a finger touching something hot. Others are triggered indirectly by special cells, called receptors, such as the photoreceptors in the eye's retina that become active when they are hit by light.

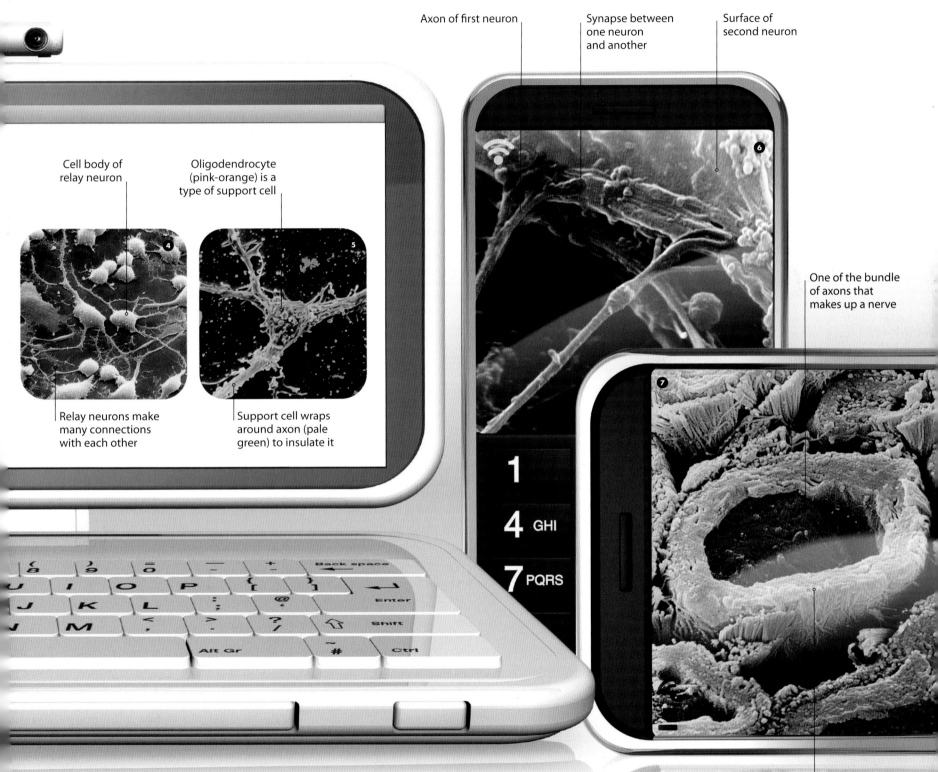

❹ RELAY NEURONS

Also called association neurons or interneurons, these nerve cells make up the majority of neurons and are only found in the brain and spinal cord. Here, they process, sort, and compare information received from sensory neurons, and issue outgoing instructions that are transmitted by motor neurons.

❻ SYNAPSE

To work as a communication network, neurons have to pass on signals to one another. Where neurons meet, at a junction called a synapse, there is a tiny gap between them. The axon of one neuron ends in a swelling called a synaptic knob. When a nerve impulse arrives, the synaptic knob releases a chemical that travels across the gap and triggers a new impulse in the dendrite of the second neuron.

Axon of first neuron

Synapse between one neuron and another

Surface of second neuron

Cell body of relay neuron

Oligodendrocyte (pink-orange) is a type of support cell

One of the bundle of axons that makes up a nerve

Relay neurons make many connections with each other

Support cell wraps around axon (pale green) to insulate it

❺ SUPPORT CELL

There are ten times as many support, or glial, cells in the nervous system as there are neurons. The job of these cells is to nurture and protect neurons. Oligodendrocytes, for example, form a fatty, insulating sheath around the axons of certain neurons, enabling them to transmit nerve impulses more rapidly. Other support cells called astrocytes supply neurons with food.

❼ NERVES

These are the "cables" of the nervous system that fan out from the brain and spinal cord and carry information back and forth between the CNS and every part of the body. Each nerve is made up of bundles of long axons and is surrounded by an outer protective coat. Most nerves carry the axons of both sensory and motor neurons.

Sheath holds bundle of axons together inside a nerve

BRAIN

Our brain is made from some 100 billion neurons, each of which form connections with hundreds or thousands of other neurons to create a massive control network. The brain consumes 20 percent of the body's energy, even though it makes up just two per cent of body weight. The largest part of the brain, the cerebrum, enables us to experience our surroundings, move in a controlled way, and to think and be self-aware. Other key parts include the cerebellum and brain stem.

❶ CEREBRAL CORTEX

The cerebrum's many tasks are performed by its thin outer layer, the cerebral cortex. Although each area of the cortex has a particular role, different areas work together. This "brain map" shows those different areas. Sensory areas receive input from receptors, motor areas send instructions to muscles, and association areas interpret and analyze information.

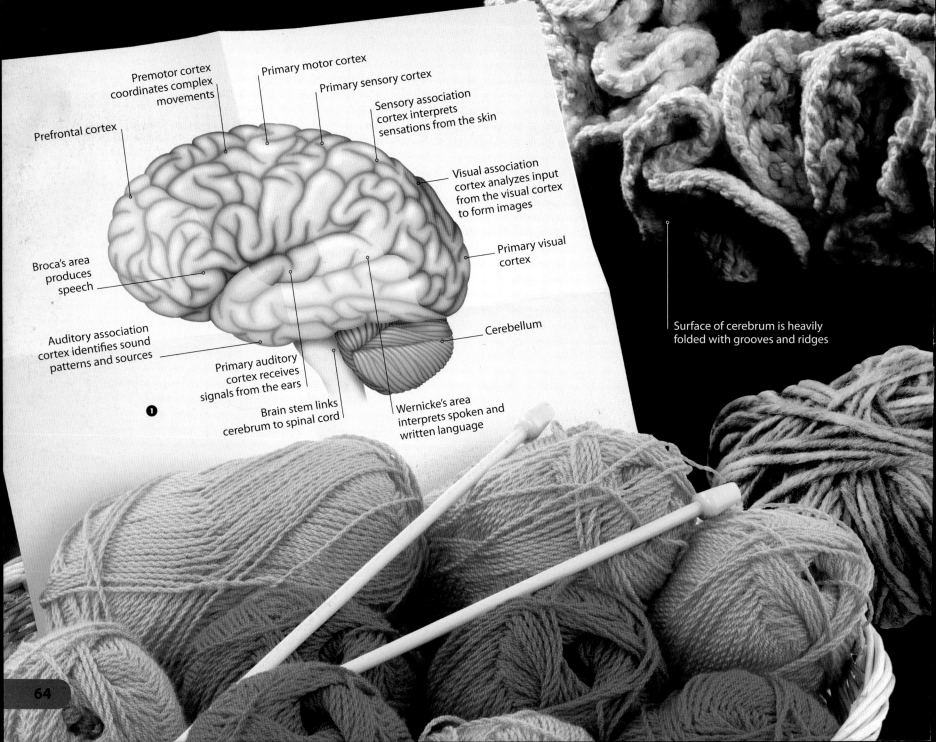

Premotor cortex coordinates complex movements

Primary motor cortex

Primary sensory cortex

Sensory association cortex interprets sensations from the skin

Prefrontal cortex

Visual association cortex analyzes input from the visual cortex to form images

Broca's area produces speech

Primary visual cortex

Auditory association cortex identifies sound patterns and sources

Cerebellum

Primary auditory cortex receives signals from the ears

❶

Brain stem links cerebrum to spinal cord

Wernicke's area interprets spoken and written language

Surface of cerebrum is heavily folded with grooves and ridges

64

❷ PREFRONTAL CORTEX

We are what we are because of this association area at the front of each side of the cerebrum. The most complex part of the brain, the prefrontal cortex gives us our personality and enables us to think and learn. It also, among other things, allows us to reason and make judgements, determines our intelligence, allows us to have abstract ideas, and gives us a conscience and the ability to care about other people.

❸ PRIMARY MOTOR CORTEX

With the help of other parts of the brain, the primary motor cortex sends out instructions to skeletal muscles that result in controlled, coordinated movements of the body. Another motor area, the neighboring premotor cortex, controls learned skills, such as riding a bike or playing the violin, by sending signals to muscles by way of the primary motor cortex. It also plays a part in planning movements.

❹ PRIMARY SENSORY CORTEX

We are able to feel our surroundings because of this area of the cortex. The primary sensory cortex receives and identifies signals from touch, pressure, heat, cold, and pain receptors in the skin, and pinpoints where the signals have come from. The sensory association area integrates input from its neighbor, and recalls previous experiences, to interpret what is being felt, in terms of shape, texture, and temperature.

Brain stem controls heart rate and breathing

Spinal cord controls many automatic actions or reflexes

❺ PRIMARY VISUAL CORTEX

This is the biggest sensory area of the cerebral cortex, reflecting the importance of vision. The primary visual cortex receives nerve impulses from the eyes and analyzes them in terms of movement, colors, and shapes. The visual association area compares these with other visual experiences so that we appreciate what we are seeing. At the same time, other parts at the back and sides of the brain tell us what we are seeing and where it is.

❻ CEREBELLUM

Making up around ten percent of the brain's weight, the cerebellum ensures that the body moves in a smooth, coordinated fashion. The cerebellum receives constant updates about the body's position and movements from stretch receptors in muscles and tendons, balance sensors in the ears, and from the eyes. It sends instructions, via the motor cortex, to skeletal muscles that control the precise timing and sequence of their contractions.

❼ SPINAL CORD

This flattened cylinder of nervous tissue extends from the base of the brain to the lower back. The spinal cord relays signals between the brain and most parts of the body, to which it is connected by 31 pairs of spinal nerves that branch out from it. More than just an information highway, the spinal cord also coordinates many automatic reflex actions without the intervention of the brain.

REFLEXES

If we touch something sharp or hot, we pull our fingers away quickly without even thinking about it, only later feeling pain. That automatic response is called a reflex. Many reflexes, including the withdrawal of hands or feet from harm, protect us from danger. Withdrawal reflexes are controlled by the spinal cord, not by the brain. Other types of reflex include the stretch reflex and reflexes found only in babies.

❶ PAIN RECEPTORS
A fingertip touches a sharp pin with sufficient force that the tip of the pin penetrates the skin. Just under the surface of the skin there are receptors that detect the pain of a pinprick. Either the tip of the pin hits the receptors, or the pin causes damage and the release of chemicals that stimulate the receptors. Either way, the receptors generate and send nerve impulses along sensory neurons.

❷ SENSORY NEURONS
These neurons carry nerve impulses from receptors, in this case pain receptors in the fingers, to the spinal cord, where they form synapses (junctions) with other neurons. The long axons, or nerve fibers, of sensory neurons, like those of motor neurons, are bundled into nerves.

❸ SPINAL CORD
This cross section through the spinal cord shows two distinct areas. The darker tissue, called white matter, around the outside is made of nerve fibers that carry signals up and down the spinal cord. The inner mass of gray matter contains relay neurons, and these pass on signals that have arrived along sensory neurons to motor neurons during a reflex action.

❹ MOTOR NEURONS

Originating in the spinal cord, motor neurons send instructions along their axons (black) to skeletal muscle fibers (red) through the nerve-muscle junctions, in order to make them contract. During this reflex, nerve signals from sensory neurons are relayed across the spinal cord to motor neurons to activate them.

❺ MUSCLE MOVEMENT

When their muscle fibers receive instructions to contract, the muscles of the upper arm rapidly get shorter and pull the forearm to jerk the hand away from danger. This takes place without a person being aware of what is going on. Only then do the nerve impulses reach the brain so that a person actually feels any pain.

Biceps brachii muscle contracts to bend arm and move hand

❻ STRETCH REFLEXES

Skeletal muscles maintain a state of partial contraction, called muscle tone, to keep us upright. Stretch reflexes, activated by stretch receptors inside muscles, constantly adjust muscle tone by making muscles tighten if they stretch too far. Doctors test the stretch reflex by tapping a tendon just below the knee, causing the thigh muscle to stretch. In response, the thigh muscle contracts and the lower leg kicks forward.

❼ NEWBORN REFLEXES

Babies are born with reflexes that aid survival. The sucking reflex, shown here, enables a newborn to suck its mother's nipple to get milk. Another reflex, the rooting instinct, makes a baby turn its head to find the nipple, when the side of its face is touched. Other reflexes include grasping, as well as holding the breath and making swimming movements underwater. These reflexes fade within the first year.

MEMORY

Being able to remember experiences is essential to our existence. Memory enables us to learn, be creative, and understand the world around us. There are three levels of memory. Sensory memory allows us for a split second to be aware of our surroundings. Short-term memory briefly holds items that we need to deal with at that moment. Long-term memory, of which there are three types, provides a lifetime store of skills, facts, and events.

Cerebral cortex

Corpus callosum links cerebral hemispheres

Thalamus filters incoming signals

Hippocampus

▲ MEMORY STORAGE

There is no single memory store in your brain. Among the key memory areas are the cerebral cortex, the outer layer of the brain's cerebral hemispheres, and the hippocampus, which is located within those hemispheres. The hippocampus constantly relays memory signals to areas of the cortex that deal with vision, hearing, and other sensations, until they store long-term memories that can be recalled.

▶ SENSORY MEMORY

Your sensory memory is in control of the moments when you are aware of your surroundings, whether you are riding a bike or watching TV. For a split second, it stores a fleeting impression of sights, sounds, smells, tastes, and other sensations before being updated. Most sensory memories are lost, to prevent the brain being overwhelmed, but any important sensations are retained in short-term memory.

◀ SHORT-TERM MEMORY
Only the most significant sensations you experience are remembered. That is the job of short-term memory, which stores things just long enough for you to act on them. For example, if you read a phone number, short-term memory retains it so you can dial it. Most short-term memories are stored for seconds then discarded, but important ones are shunted to long-term memory.

▶ PROCEDURAL MEMORY

One of the three types of long-term memory, procedural memory is located deep inside your brain. It stores all those skills that people learn through practice, from the most basic, such as walking, to more complex, such as being able to play a piano. Once learned, procedural memory makes sure these skills and "how to" knowledge are rarely lost.

▶ SEMANTIC MEMORY
The reason you can read these words and make sense of what they mean is because of your semantic memory. Located in the sides of the cerebrum, semantic memory stores the words and language you have learned since infancy, both inside and out of school, along with lots of facts and their meanings. It helps you understand what is in front of you.

EPISODIC MEMORY ▶

Remembering a great holiday or your first day at school depends on episodic memory. Located in different parts of the cerebral cortex, such as those responsible for vision and hearing, episodic memory stores specific life events. One way to "jog" your episodic memory is to look at photographs. These can "switch on" parts of the cortex, so they recreate the event.

◀ MAKING MEMORIES

While most sensations last just a few seconds, some, such as the sights, sounds, and smells of this carnival, can make a big impression. Received from short-term memory, these sensations are processed by the hippocampus and eventually pass into long-term memory in the cerebral cortex. Here, nerve cells create new connections with each other to create a "memory web", in which memories can be stored and then recalled over a lifetime.

SLEEP

Every day of our lives we experience two quite different states of existence—being fully awake and conscious, and being asleep. Sleep is a state of altered consciousness from which we can be woken. The brain is still active, especially during REM sleep, but our thoughts are generally cut off from the world around us. Why we sleep is not fully understood, although being deprived of sleep makes us ill. Sleep certainly allows the body to rest and gives the brain "down time" when it processes the previous day's experiences, and commits certain significant events to memory.

BRAIN WAVES ▶

When brain cells communicate with each other, they create a "chatter" of electrical signals, called brain waves, that can be detected and turned into patterns, called electroencephalograms (EEG), as shown here. EEGs show that there are four basic types of brain waves—beta, alpha, theta, and delta. Beta waves are produced when we are awake and alert. The other types of brain waves occur at different stages of sleep.

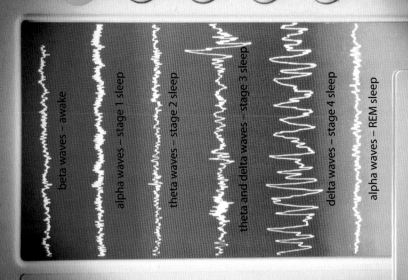

beta waves – awake

alpha waves – stage 1 sleep

theta waves – stage 2 sleep

theta and delta waves – stage 3 sleep

delta waves – stage 4 sleep

alpha waves – REM sleep

◀ RELAXED MUSCLES

When we are awake some of our muscles—especially in the neck, back, and legs—remain partially contracted. This partial contraction, called muscle tone, maintains posture by supporting our body and keeping it upright. When we sleep, muscle tone all but disappears. This is most obvious in someone who nods off in a chair. Their head lolls forward or to the side, and their body becomes floppy.

YAWNING ▶

When a person yawns, the mouth opens wide and a deep breath is taken. We generally yawn when we are tired or bored, but why yawning happens is still a mystery. Yawning was believed to "flush out" excess carbon dioxide from the lungs, but scientists now question that. Another suggestion is that yawning helps to cool an overheated brain. Whatever its purpose, yawning is contagious. If one person starts, others soon follow.

◀ AMOUNT OF SLEEP

We spend around one-third of our lives asleep, but the amount of sleep we need each night decreases as we get older. Newborn babies sleep for up to 18 hours a day, although tired parents may not appreciate that. Children need 11 hours on average, a figure that decreases to around ten hours for teenagers. Young adults average eight hours a night, while older people may only need five or six hours sleep each night.

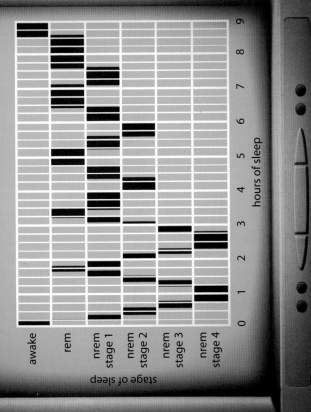

▲ SLEEP PATTERNS

A typical night's sleep follows a regular pattern. Initially, a sleeper moves through four stages of deep sleep, or NREM (non-rapid eye movement), during which brain activity decreases sharply. This is followed by REM (rapid eye movement) sleep, when the brain is active and dreaming occurs, but muscles—apart from those moving the eyes—become "paralyzed". This cycle of NREM and REM sleep is repeated through the night with the proportion of REM sleep increasing until it's time to wake up.

hours of sleep

stage of sleep

awake
rem
nrem stage 1
nrem stage 2
nrem stage 3
nrem stage 4

0 1 2 3 4 5 6 7 8 9

▶ SLEEP STUDY

Why we sleep and how sleep works are not entirely clear. The subject has fascinated scientists and psychologists for many years. One way of studying sleep is to record the electrical activity of millions of brain neurons as they transmit signals. Electrical activity is detected by attaching electrodes to the skin of the scalp and face. Those electrodes are connected by wires to an electroencephalograph, a machine that converts electrical signals into patterns called brain waves.

Electrode attached to skin detects electrical activity of brain neurons

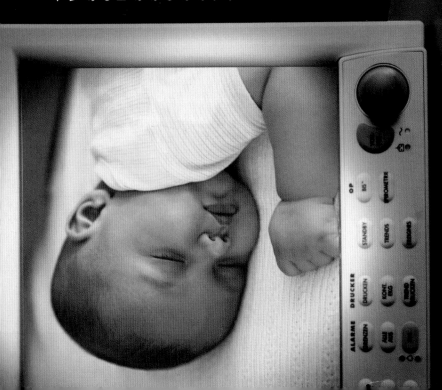

VISION

Our most important sense, vision provides the brain with massive amounts of information about our surroundings. The eyes, which are protected within bony orbits in the skull and by the eyelids and tears, contain around 70 percent of the body's sensory receptors. They act like digital cameras, automatically focusing light and controlling the amount of light entering them. They then send signals to the brain, which creates the images that we "see."

◀ TEARS

The front of the eye is constantly cleaned and moistened by tears produced by a gland just under the eyebrow, and spread across the eye by blinking. As well as washing away dust, tears contain lysozyme, a substance that kills bacteria. Tear production increases to wash away irritants, such as onion vapors, or when someone is feeling tearfully sad or happy.

Eye chart used to test the eyes' focusing abilities

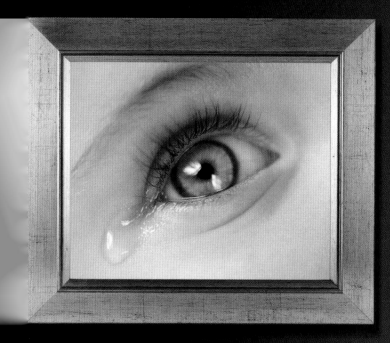

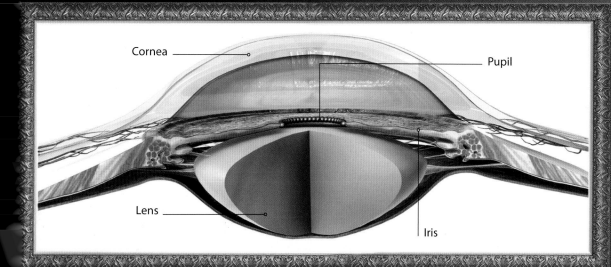

Cornea

Pupil

Lens

Iris

▲ FOCUSING LIGHT

This cross section through the front of the eye shows the cornea and the lens that lies behind it. Light rays reflected from, or produced by, the object you are looking at are focused by both cornea and lens to produce a sharp image on the retina. The elastic lens changes shape so it can focus light from both near and distant objects.

◄ IRIS AND PUPIL

The colored part of the eye, the iris (orange), surrounds the pupil (blue), the opening that allows light into the back of the eye. In bright light, tiny muscles in the iris make the pupil smaller to cut the amount of light entering the eye and prevent dazzling. In dim light, they make the pupil wider to let in more light. This automatic reflex action ensures that the eyes can work in a wide range of light intensities.

RETINA ►

The rear of the eye is lined by a thin layer called the retina. This is packed with light-detecting cells or photoreceptors of two types, as shown in this micrograph. Around 120 million rods (pink) work best in dim light and "see" in black and white. Some six million cones (green) work best in bright light and give us color vision.

▼ VISUAL CORTEX

"Seeing" happens in the visual cortex at the back of the brain's cerebrum. When light hits the retina, it sends signals along the optic nerve. Signals from the right side of each retina go to the right visual cortex, and those from the left go to the left visual cortex. Here, signals are interpreted, compared, and turned into moving, 3-D images.

▼ EYE MOVEMENTS

The eyes are constantly on the move. When looking at static objects, they make small, rapid movements called saccades to scan all parts of the scene. They also make larger, smoother movements to track objects that are on the go. These precise eye movements are produced by six straplike muscles anchored to the bony orbit.

Optic nerve

Brain

Right visual cortex

Eye

Retina

Lens

Superior rectus moves eye upward

Lateral rectus pulls eye to the side

Superior oblique moves eye downward and outward

Inferior rectus makes eye look downward

Inferior oblique moves eye upward and outward

Medial rectus moves eye inward

Left visual cortex

HEARING

From the dropping of a pin to the roar of a jet, we use our sense of hearing to detect sound. Some sounds give us pleasure, others let us communicate, while a few warn us of danger. Sounds are created by sources that vibrate and send pressure waves through the air. These waves are detected by the ears. The ears send signals to the brain, where they are analyzed and compared with sounds we have heard before, so we can readily identify what we are listening to.

▶ EAR STRUCTURE

What we generally refer to as the ear is its outer part, the pinna, which directs sound waves into the rest of the ear. The rest of the ear lies concealed and protected within the skull. An outer ear canal carries sounds to the eardrum. Its vibrations are converted into movements of the three ossicles that straddle the middle ear. These then send pressure waves through the fluid filling the coiled cochlea inside the inner ear, and this sends signals to the brain.

Cochlear nerve

Ossicles (ear bones)

Cochlea

Eustachian tube

Eardrum

Cartilage

Outer ear canal

Pinna or ear flap

▼ HAIR CELLS

This micrograph shows rows of U-shaped "hairs" (left) sprouting from some of the 15,000 sound-detecting hair cells (right) in the cochlea. Incoming sounds send waves rippling through the fluid filling the cochlea. These waves bend the "hairs", causing their hair cells to generate signals that travel along nerve fibers that make up the cochlear nerve. This carries the signals to the brain, where they are interpreted as recognizable sounds.

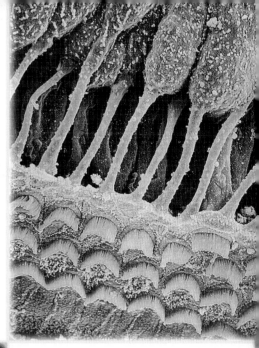

▲ OSSICLES

Three tiny bones called ossicles, linked by synovial joints, extend across the middle ear, carrying sound vibrations from the eardrum to the inner ear. The ossicles are named the hammer (nearest the eardrum), anvil, and stirrup, according to their shapes. When the eardrum vibrates, the ossicles move back and forth, the stirrup bone acting like a piston to set up vibrations inside the fluid-filled inner ear.

Incus (anvil)

Malleus (hammer)

Stapes (stirrup)

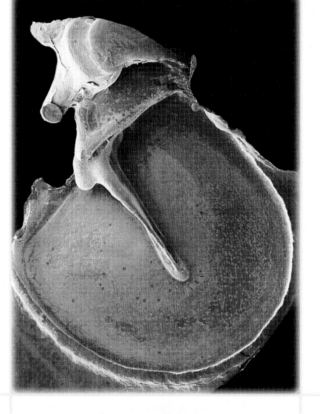

▲ EARDRUM

As taut as a drum skin, this thin membrane covers the end of the ear canal and separates it from the middle ear. When sound waves reach the inner end of the ear canal they make the eardrum vibrate. The eardrum, in turn, passes on the vibrations to the ossicles. Here, you can see the inner surface of the eardrum (red) with the hammer, one of the ossicles, attached.

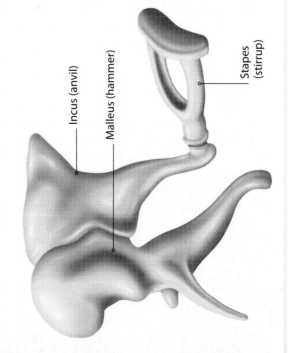

▼ SOUND FREQUENCIES

How high or low a sound is is called its pitch and it depends on the sound's frequency. This is how quickly one sound wave follows the next. Frequency is measured in hertz (Hz). Young adults can hear sounds in the range 20 Hz (low frequency and pitch) to 20,000 Hz. That range decreases as we age, especially at higher frequencies. Bats use high-pitched sounds to navigate and catch prey, and can detect frequencies up to 120,000 Hz that are completely inaudible to us.

▶ EUSTACHIAN TUBE

If air pressure inside the middle ear is not the same as that outside the body the eardrum does not vibrate freely, so hearing fades. Air pressures inside and out are equalized by the Eustachian tube that connects the middle ear with the throat. If outside pressure changes suddenly, for example inside a plane that is taking off, yawning or swallowing can open the flattened tube to equalize pressures; an action that makes the ears "pop."

BALANCE

Every time we stand up and move, the body over. What keeps us when we fall over. This keeps us when we becomes this happening and liable to balance. This becomes unstable and liable to balance. This run. Unlike vision, body. In posture to stop us falling over. Instead, of the body. In posture in posture becomes stops when we stand still and stops us falling over. upright vision, receptors. In response to stop us falling over. from one set of receptors and movements adjustments about that make the constant adjustments muscles that make us upright.

◉ BRAIN

The cerebellum receives a stream of information about the body's movements in the ears. These detect about the receptors in the head and the speed and the position of its movements detect that stretching, "see" space position of its movements that the eyes that "see" direction in muscles that are also sent by "feel" our posture. receptors is also sent by "feel" motor cortex Information touch receptors cerebellum muscles, if we and touch receptors cerebellum muscles, carefully send instructions the skeletal muscles so that, if we In response contractions so that, if we send instructions that they immediately tighten controlling their contractions, they immediately tighten start to fall over, they and pull us upright.

Motor cortex sends instructions to muscles

Sensory cortex receives messages from receptors

Cerebellum coordinates muscle contraction

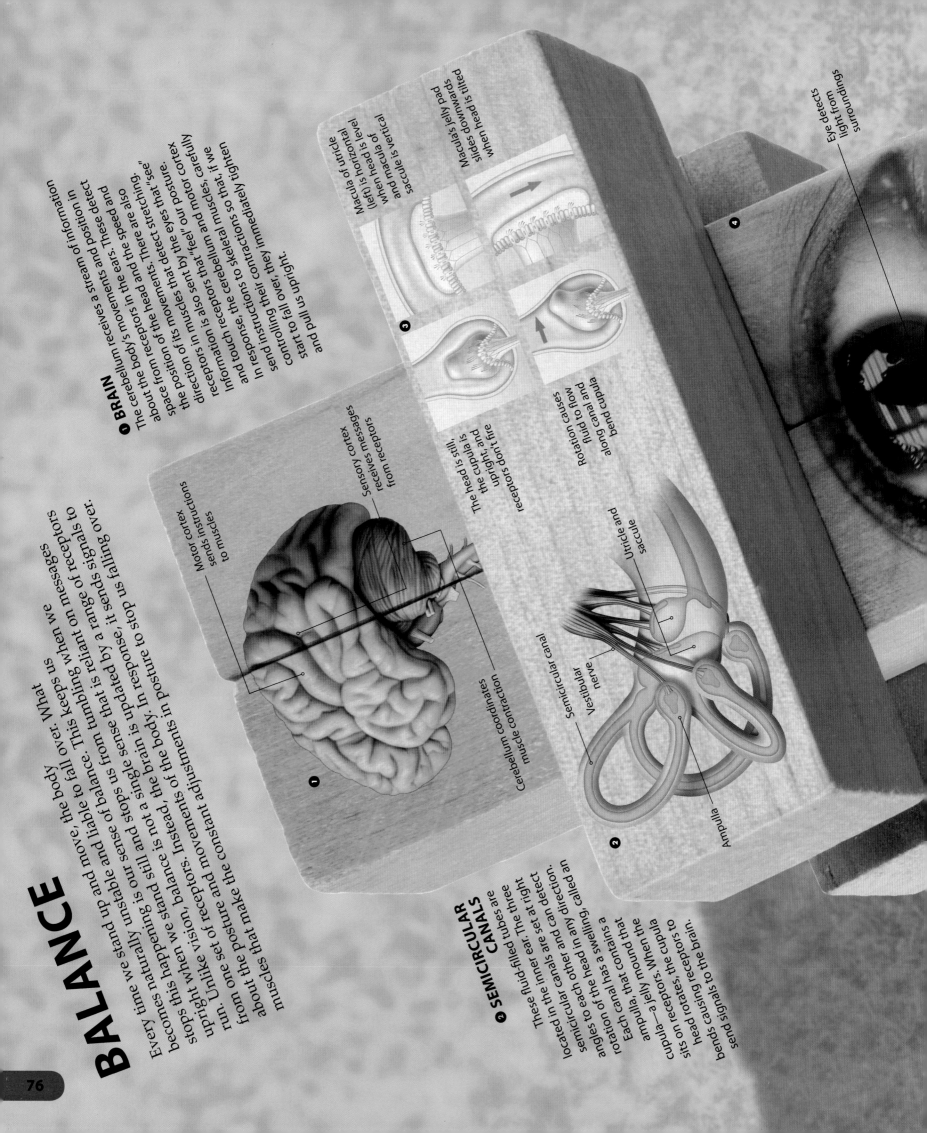

Macula of utricle (left) is horizontal when head is level when head of and macula of saccule is vertical

Macula's jelly pad slides downwards when head is tilted

The head is still, the cupula is upright, and upright receptors don't fire

Rotation causes fluid to flow along canal and bend cupula

Utricle and saccule

Semicircular canal

Vestibular nerve

Ampulla

Eye detects light from surroundings

◉ SEMICIRCULAR CANALS

These fluid-filled tubes are located in the inner ear. The three semicircular canals and can detect a semicircular other and in any direction, called an angles of the head in any direction. A rotation canal has a swelling, called an Each canal has contains a ampulla, that contains that cupula—a jelly mound that sits on receptors, the cupula head rotates, the cupula to bends causing receptors to send signals to the brain.

❸ VESTIBULE
This part of the inner ear contains two balance organs, the utricle and saccule. Each contains a macula—a patch of weighted jelly. Any project line acceleration in a lift, or accelerating straight line going up in jelly and the the head—causes the jelly to slip and the in a car—causes the saccule to the brain. the utricle to send signals to the brain. receptors to send signals to the brain.

❹ EYES
Sensory input from the eyes plays an important part in balance. Visual clues are interpreted or moving, and help it to work out whether the body is upright and help it to work out whether other signals can lead to confusion—which signals clues and on a ship. Then—they may conflict that the body is a person is on a ship. Then—may indicate in motion sickness. that the body receptors. This can result in motion sickness. from up and down. This can result in motion sickness. moving up and down.

❺ STRETCH RECEPTORS
Found inside muscles and stretched these receptors detect how the muscle a muscle or tendon is when the muscle contracts. Stretch brain about muscle messages to the as the muscle, responds length and tension, in turn, to the muscle to stretches. The brain, in muscle to the stretching. with instructions to avoid receptors contract to avoid overstretching. In this way, stretch with lots provide way, the brain with the body's information about the body's position and posture.

❻ TOUCH RECEPTORS
Whenever we stand up, our body exerts a downward force—its weight— on our feet, and the ground touch and exerts a down this is the ground. This upward force from squeezes the underside pressure distorts on the underside, running, force receptors on walking, pressures of jumping, different it about the of the feet, and they send it about or jumping all apply, and to update the to these the brain to update the signals to the feet and how the signals to the body's position of the feet and how the body is moving.

Stretch receptors in some muscle fibers detect how they are stretched.

Receptor in skin detects touch and pressure

Muscle fibers contract to hold position or move position of body

77

TASTE AND SMELL

Our senses of taste and smell work in very similar ways. Both detect dissolved substances using receptors located in the tongue, for taste, and in the nose, for smell. Together, they enable us to enjoy the smells of our surroundings, and the flavours of food and drink. However, this is an unequal partnership, with smell being around 10,000 times more sensitive than taste. These senses also provide us with an early warning of danger, be it a nasty taste or a suspicious smell.

○ TONGUE'S SURFACE

Look at the surface of your tongue in a mirror and you will see that it is covered with lots of small bumps. These are called papillae, two types of which can be seen in this close-up micrograph of the tongue's surface. Mushroom-shaped fungiform papillae house the taste buds that detect different tastes in food and drink. Spiky filiform papillae lack taste buds, but they also play an important role as they help the tongue grip food during chewing. The tongue has special receptors for heat and cold, and pain receptors that detect the "heat" of spicy food such as chillies.

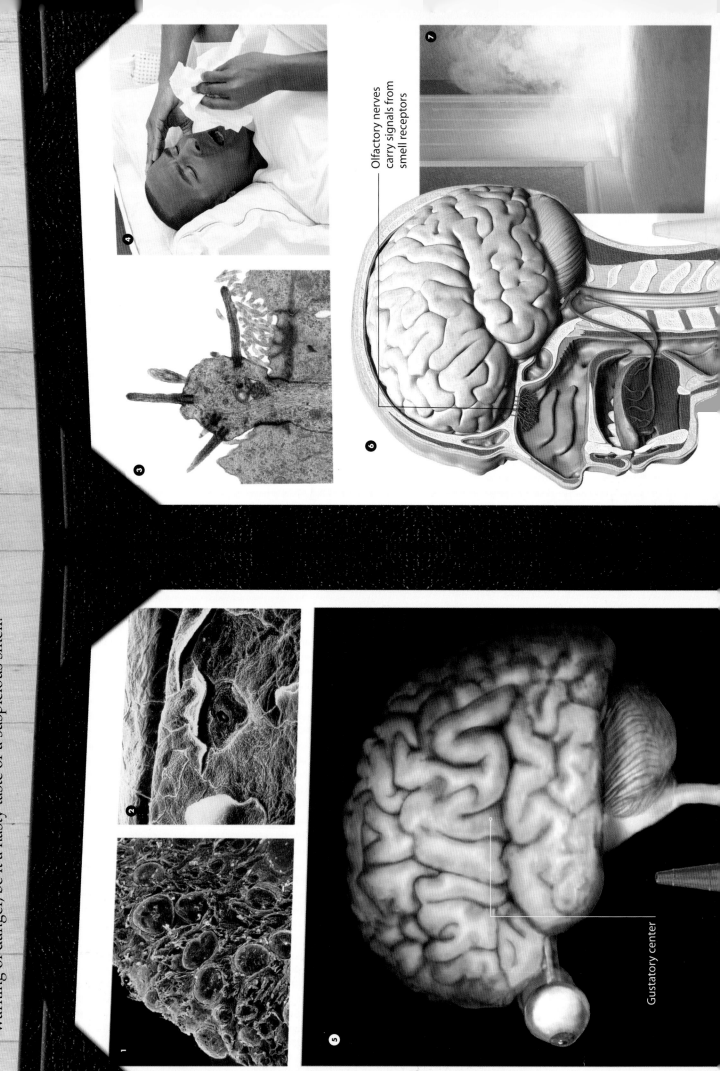

Olfactory nerves carry signals from smell receptors

Gustatory center

❷ TASTE BUDS

The tongue's 10,000 or so taste buds detect just five basic tastes—sweet, sour, salty, bitter, and umami (a meaty taste). Taste buds are housed in the top and sides of some of the tongue's papillae. This micrograph shows a taste pore in a papilla that opens into a taste bud, which contains receptor cells. When you eat, taste molecules in food dissolve in saliva, pass through the taste pore, and are detected by the receptors. Signals are sent from the receptors to the brain's taste center, where the taste information is processed.

❸ SMELL RECEPTORS

Millions of smell receptors are located in the upper part of your nasal cavity. The tip of a receptor, shown in this micrograph (red), projects into the nasal cavity and carries between ten and 20 hairlike cilia. When you breathe in through your nose, odor molecules in the air dissolve in watery mucus covering the cilia. Dissolved odor molecules bind to the cilia, which causes smell receptors to send signals to the brain, where individual odors are identified. Smell receptors are very sensitive and can pick up a wide range of scents—in all, they can detect over 10,000 different odors.

❹ WORKING TOGETHER

Whenever we eat or drink, our senses of smell and taste work together. Smell, being much more sensitive than taste, works as the "senior partner" in this relationship. If, like the man in the picture, we have a cold, thick mucus in the nasal cavity stops us from smelling normally. As a result, any food we eat tastes bland, with little flavor.

❺ TASTE CENTER

Whether we taste food as being sweet, sour, salty, bitter, or meaty—or a combination of some or all of these—depends on the brain's gustatory or taste centers. It's here that the brain processes signals from the taste buds that identify tastes. En route to the gustatory area these signals also stimulate the release of saliva and stomach juices, which play key roles in digestion.

❻ TASTE AND SMELL NERVES

This cross section through the head shows the routes taken by signals from smell receptors in the nasal cavity and taste buds in the tongue. Smell signals travel along olfactory nerves to the front of the brain where odors are interpreted. Two nerves carry taste signals from the tongue to the brain's gustatory areas.

❼ EARLY WARNING

Our sense of smell can provide early warning of dangers. Just one whiff of smoke or natural gas (a substance is added to this otherwise odorless gas to make it smelly), makes us alert to possible harm and may trigger the body's fight or flight response. This instantly prepares us to either confront danger or run away from it. The presence of unpleasant smells may also trigger defensive reflexes such as sneezing.

❽ BAD TASTES

We have a built-in, protective dislike for foods that taste bitter or sour, especially as children. This is because bitterness or sourness often indicate that food is poisonous or rotten. Detecting such tastes while food is still in the mouth means we can take evasive action by spitting it out. That said, we learn to enjoy bitter-tasting foods, such as olives and coffee, and benefit from sour-tasting fruits, such as lemons, which are rich in vitamins.

TOUCH

Skin is a sense organ. Scattered throughout it are receptors that give us our sense of touch, a sense that keeps us constantly informed about our surroundings. A cold breeze hitting the skin, the soft feel of a cat's fur, or the pain of a paper cut are just some of the physical sensations we experience using this sense. There are several different types of receptor in the skin, and each responds to a different stimulus. When processed by the brain, signals from these receptors together give us a touch "picture" of the world around us.

▶ TOUCH RECEPTORS

The majority of touch receptors are located in the dermis, the thicker, lower layer of the skin, although some extend into the thinner epidermis. Most are mechanoreceptors, receptors that send signals to the brain when they are physically squashed or pulled. Smaller mechanoreceptors near the skin's surface detect light touch, while larger, deeper ones pick up pressure and stretching. Some receptors detect temperature changes, while others detect chemicals released when the skin is damaged, and send messages to the brain about pain.

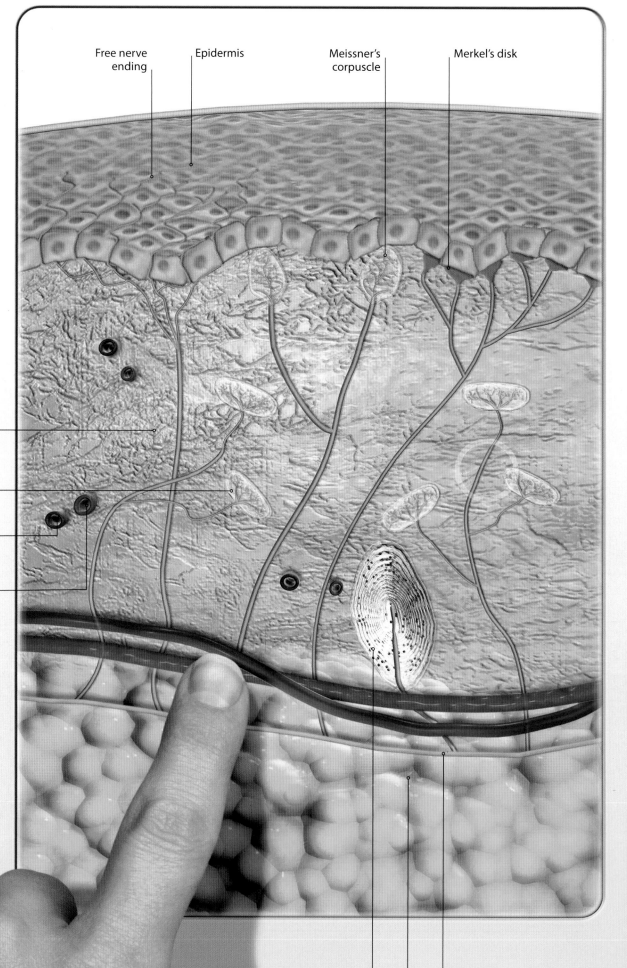

Free nerve ending

Epidermis

Meissner's corpuscle

Merkel's disk

Dermis

Ruffini's corpuscle

Cross section of vein

Cross section of artery

Pacinian corpuscle

Nerve

Subcutaneous fat

▶ FREE NERVE ENDINGS

Step into a hot shower or dive into a freezing pool and you feel the sudden change in temperature thanks to free nerve endings in your skin. These act as thermoreceptors, receptors that react to heat and cold. Other free nerve endings act as nociceptors, receptors that enable you to feel pain. Free nerve endings have no capsules around the tips and extend into the epidermis itself.

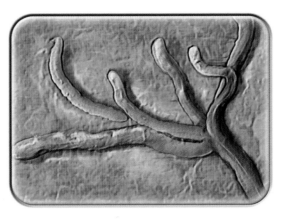

▶ MEISSNER'S CORPSUCLE

Located near the junction of the dermis and epidermis, these egg-shaped receptors consist of branching nerve endings surrounded by a capsule. Meissner's corpuscles are common in sensitive, hairless skin, such as on the fingertips, palms, soles, eyelids, lips, and nipples. They are sensitive to light touch and pressure, and allow us to identify objects by their size, shape, and texture.

▶ MERKEL'S DISK

Lying close to the surface of the skin, Merkel's disks consist of branched nerve endings associated with specialized disk-shaped cells called Merkel's cells in the bottom layer of the epidermis. Merkel's disks detect light pressure and touch. In the skin of the fingertips, these detectors can distinguish between the texture of velvet and of sandpaper.

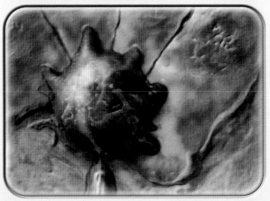

▶ PACINIAN CORPUSCLE

Deep in the dermis these big, egg-shaped receptors detect "on-off" pressure and vibrations. The Pacinian corpuscle's nerve ending is surrounded by layers of flattened cells, so in section it looks a bit like a cut onion. A sudden change in pressure on the skin squashes the receptor and stimulates its nerve ending to send signals to the brain.

▶ RUFFINI'S CORPUSCLE

A branching array of nerve endings surrounded by a flat capsule, Ruffini's corpuscles detect deep, continuous pressure and stretching of the skin. In the hands, they detect the sliding movements of objects across the skin's surface, helping the fingers to grip those objects. They are similar to receptors in tendons that monitor muscle stretching.

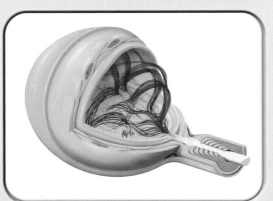

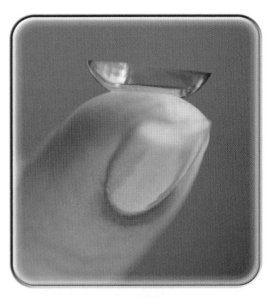

▲ SENSITIVE FINGERS

Sensory receptors are not distributed evenly throughout the skin. Your fingertips have lots more touch, pressure, and vibration receptors than most other parts of the body. This makes them incredibly sensitive so that they can detect the lightest touch and distinguish the texture of the object they are touching, such as this contact lens.

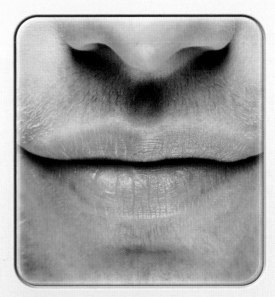

▲ SENSITIVE LIPS

Your lips are very sensitive because, like the fingers, they are packed with touch receptors. The part of the brain that processes signals from these receptors is called the sensory cortex. Much larger parts of the sensory cortex are dedicated to dealing with signals from sensitive body areas than from less sensitive parts, such as the back of the elbows and knees.

Pituitary gland is raisin-sized and positioned below the brain

Scan of the brain from the front shows the hypothalamus at its centre

Ovary

Left kidney

Adrenal gland sits on top of the kidney

HORMONES

Two body systems control and coordinate its activities. The nervous system uses electrical signals and works rapidly. The endocrine, or hormonal, system usually operates more slowly, with longer term effects on processes, including growth and reproduction. The endocrine system consists of a number of glands that release chemical messengers called hormones into the blood. Hormones target specific cells or tissues and change their activities. Once their work is done, hormones are destroyed by the liver.

❶ Pituitary gland and hypothalamus

The pituitary gland releases nine hormones that help regulate metabolic rate, growth, and reproduction. Many of these hormones trigger other endocrine organs to release hormones of their own. The pituitary gland is itself controlled by the brain's hypothalamus. This makes hormones that either stimulate the pituitary gland to release hormones, or are released by the pituitary itself. This connection between the hypothalamus and the pituitary gland links the nervous and endocrine systems.

❷ Adrenal glands

The outer parts of adrenal glands release more than 20 hormones called corticosteroids. The inner parts work with the autonomic nervous system by releasing the hormone adrenaline, also called epinephrine. This acts to prepare the body for danger by increasing heart and breathing rates.

❸ Ovaries

A woman's ovaries release an egg each month and the female sex hormones estrogen and progesterone. Oestrogen maintains female characteristics such as body shape and breasts. It works with progesterone to control the menstrual cycle, which prepares the uterus to receive a fertilized egg.

❹ Pancreas

As well as releasing digestive enzymes into the small intestine, the pancreas also produces two hormones, insulin and glucagon, that keep glucose—the body's energy supply—at a fairly constant level in the bloodstream.

❺ Thymus gland

At its biggest and most important during childhood, the thymus gland is found beneath the sternum (breastbone). It releases hormones that encourage cells called T lymphocytes to develop normally and become active. T lymphocytes play a key part in the immune system that defends the body against disease. During adult life, the thymus gradually shrinks.

❻ Pineal gland

Situated near the brain's center, the pineal gland releases melatonin, a hormone that helps to control sleeping and waking.

❼ Thyroid and parathyroid glands

Located in the front of the neck, the thyroid gland releases two hormones. Thyroxine stimulates body cells to increase their metabolic rate, while calcitonin inhibits the release of calcium from bones. The hormone PTH, released from four tiny parathyroid glands, has the opposite effect to calcitonin.

❽ Testes

As well as producing sperm, the two testes also release the male sex hormone testosterone. This stimulates sperm production and maintains male features, such as a muscular body shape, deep voice, and facial and body hair. Testosterone release is controlled by a pituitary gland hormone.

Pineal gland

Thyroid gland
Parathyroid gland

EMERGENCY

Our bodies can cope with many different situations, and emergencies are no exception. Confronted by any sort of threat or stress, a built-in mechanism speeds into action to prepare the body to deal with the problem. Aided by the hormone adrenaline, also called epinephrine, the autonomic nervous system (ANS) targets the heart, lungs, liver, and other body parts to get extra oxygen and fuel to the brain and muscles. Once primed for action, the body can either confront the emergency or run away from it. This is the fight-or-flight reaction.

▲ SCARY SITUATIONS

Stressful or alarming situations include the fear and excitement generated by a roller coaster ride, or the sheer terror induced by being chased through the woods by a bear, or the stress of being stuck in a traffic jam when you want to get somewhere. These situations will make the body marshal its resources using the ANS and adrenaline in order to confront the threat, real or imaginary, or escape from it.

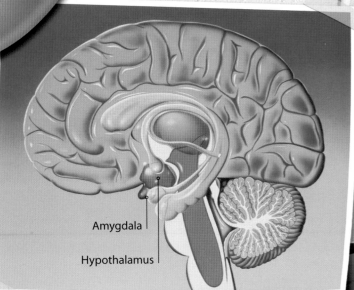

Amygdala

Hypothalamus

▲ AMYGDALA

The amygdala is part of the limbic system—the brain's emotional center. When a person sees or imagines something that is scary or threatening, signals from the eyes, ears, or parts of the brain zip along nerve fibers to the amygdala. This, in turn, alerts its neighbor, the hypothalamus, a small but vitally important part of the brain.

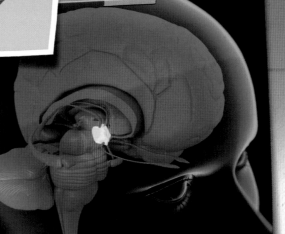

◄ HYPOTHALAMUS

In charge of regulating so many body activities, the hypothalamus performs a lot of its roles through the ANS. When it receives fear signals from the amygdala, it activates a part of the ANS called the sympathetic division, which has the effect of rousing the body into action. The hypothalamus sends out signals along sympathetic motor neurons to various body parts, including the adrenal glands.

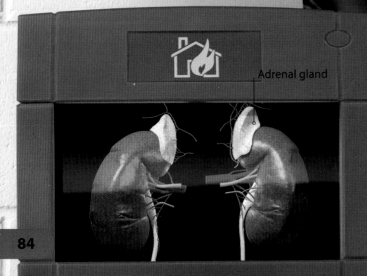

Adrenal gland

◄ ADRENAL GLANDS

Triggered by nerve impulses arriving from the hypothalamus, each adrenal gland swings into action at the first sign of an emergency. The central medulla of the adrenal gland pours quantities of the hormone adrenaline into the bloodstream. Adrenaline reinforces the actions of the ANS by, for example, targeting the heart, to make it beat faster, or the liver, to release glucose.

◄ HEART

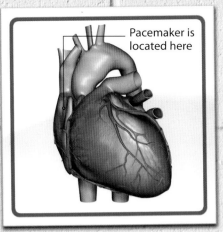

Pacemaker is located here

Anyone who's been scared will recognize the familiar feeling of a pounding heart. In scary situations, the ANS and adrenaline target the pacemaker and other parts of the heart to increase the rate and force of heartbeats. This ensures that more blood gets to muscles and the brain, where it delivers vital oxygen and fuel.

◄ LUNGS

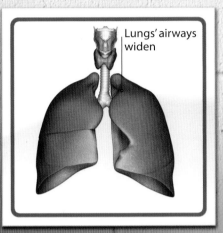

Lungs' airways widen

Each lung contains a massive network of airways. The largest, called bronchi, divide into smaller bronchioles, the smallest of which carry air into and out of the alveoli, or air sacs, through which oxygen enters the blood. During an emergency, tiny muscles wrapped around the bronchioles relax. They widen and carry more air to the alveoli, so that extra oxygen gets into the bloodstream.

◄ LIVER

Among its many roles, the liver stores glucose. This energy-rich sugar is kept in liver cells in the form of a complex carbohydrate called glycogen. During an emergency, demand for glucose soars. The ANS and adrenaline stimulate liver cells to break down glycogen into glucose and release it into the bloodstream. It is then transported to where it is needed most, notably the brain and muscles.

Liver releases glucose

▼ WIDE PUPILS

Look into the eyes of someone who is scared and the combined effects of the ANS and adrenaline are obvious. Together, they cause the contraction of tiny muscle fibers in the iris, the colored part of the eye, that make its central pupil really wide. This lets extra light into the eyes, giving someone a better view of what is happening around them.

◄ CHANGING BLOOD FLOW

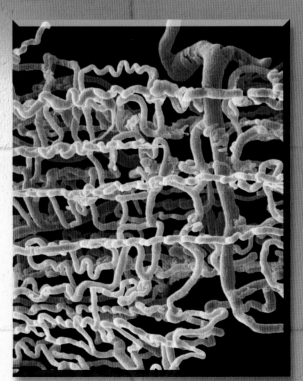

In an emergency situation, digestion is not a priority. Blood vessels supplying the digestive system narrow to reduce blood flow. The same applies to the skin, making a frightened person go pale. Blood diverted from the digestive system and skin goes to the brain, to increase alertness, and to muscles. Blood vessels inside muscles widen, vastly increasing blood flow to muscle cells, giving them extra energy to confront any threat.

LIFE BLOOD
A legion of red blood cells inside a blood vessel travel swiftly around the body to deliver essential oxygen to its trillions of cells. This is just one of many processes that cooperate to maintain the body.

Maintenance

BLOOD

To stay alive, body cells need constant deliveries of oxygen, food, and other essentials, and removal of waste. This service is provided by the blood, a red liquid that courses along blood vessels, pumped by the heart. Together, the blood, blood vessels, and heart make up the circulatory system. Blood consists of red and white blood cells and platelets floating in a yellowish liquid called plasma. Plasma carries out most of the roles of blood including transporting food and wastes. Red blood cells carry oxygen, white blood cells fight infection, and platelets help repair damaged blood vessels.

▶ HEMOGLOBIN
Around 250 million molecules of hemoglobin, the orangey-red protein that gives blood its color, are packed into every red blood cell. Hemoglobin picks up oxygen in the lungs, then releases it where it's needed, in the tissues. As it does this, hemoglobin changes color, making oxygen-rich blood bright red and oxygen-poor blood dark red. Each hemoglobin molecule carries four oxygen molecules, so one red blood cell can transport one billion oxygen molecules.

▶ PLATELETS
A damaged blood vessel leaking blood could prove life-threatening. To stem leaks, the circulatory system has a self-repair mechanism in which platelets play a key role. Around one-third the size of a red blood cell, platelets are cell fragments. If a blood vessel is damaged, platelets congregate at the site and become "sticky." The resulting mass of platelets forms a temporary plug that stops blood loss and sets clotting in motion.

▶ CLOTTING
As the platelets stem blood loss from a broken blood vessel, they trigger the next stage in the mending process—clotting. Sticky platelets release chemicals that convert the blood protein fibrinogen into threads of fibrin. At the wound site, entangled fibrin fibers act like a net to trap blood cells and form a jellylike clot. A stronger, more permanent structure than the platelet plug, the clot remains in place, gradually shrinking, until tissue repair is complete.

Hemoglobin molecule binds oxygen

Neutrophils track down and eat pathogens

Fibrin threads trap blood cells to form a clot

Platelets are cell fragments rather than whole cells

A small drop of blood contains
an incredible 250 million red
blood cells. Red blood cells
are unique because they
have no nucleus, being
filled instead with oxygen-
carrying hemoglobin.
Their dimpled disk shape
is ideal for taking up and
releasing oxygen really
efficiently. They are also
small and very flexible,
enabling them to squeeze
along the smallest capillaries
to unload oxygen supplies to
demanding tissue cells. Red blood
cells wear out after around 120 days,
when they are recycled.

▼ **WHITE BLOOD CELLS**
Although outnumbered by red blood cells 700 to
one, white blood cells still have a vital role to play.
They destroy bacteria and other disease-causing
pathogens that invade the body. There are several
different kinds of white blood cell, including
neutrophils, monocytes, and lymphocytes. White
blood cells, unlike red cells, can squeeze through
the walls of capillaries to track down prey. It's
here that monocytes transform into voracious
pathogen-eating cells called macrophages.

Lymphocytes release
antibodies, chemicals
that mark pathogens
for destruction

Debris inside blood
vessel must be removed
to prevent blockages

Macrophage
bending and
to "eat" a
piece of debris

❶ CIRCULATORY SYSTEM

Here are the circulatory system's major arteries and veins—the capillaries that link them are too small to see. Circulating blood follows two loops. In one loop, oxygen-poor blood travels along the pulmonary arteries to the lungs to pick up oxygen, and oxygen-rich blood travels back to the heart along the pulmonary veins. In the other, oxygen-rich blood travels along the carotid, femoral, and other arteries to the body, and oxygen-poor blood returns through the jugular, tibial, and other veins towards the heart.

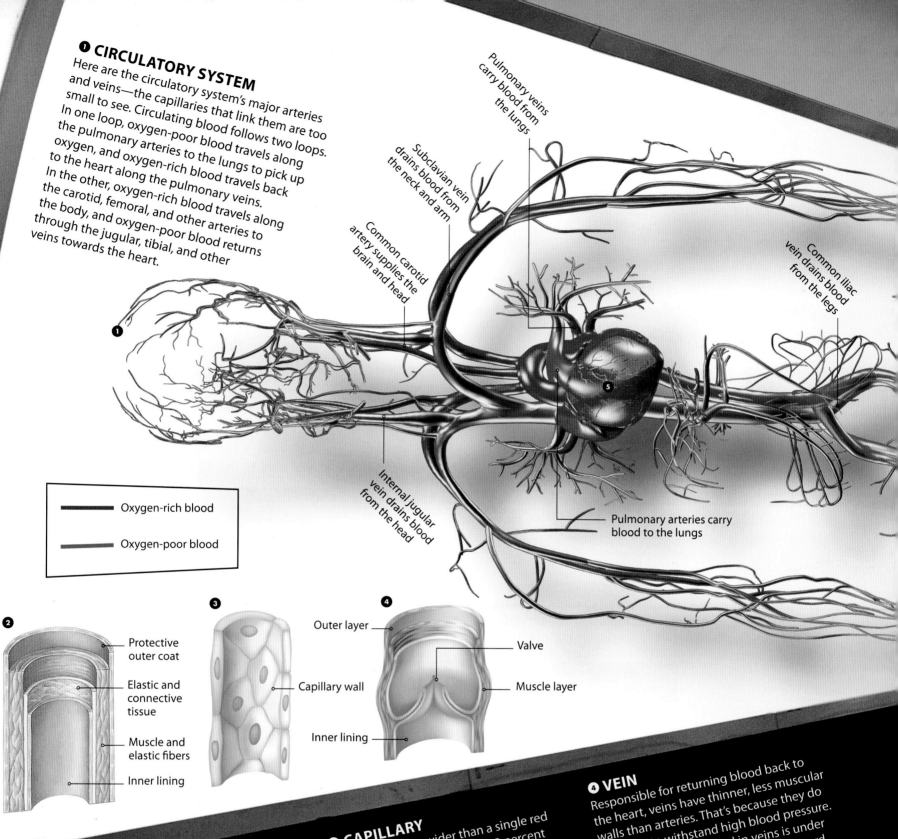

Pulmonary veins carry blood from the lungs

Subclavian vein drains blood from the neck and arm

Common carotid artery supplies the brain and head

Common iliac vein drains blood from the legs

Internal jugular vein drains blood from the head

Pulmonary arteries carry blood to the lungs

▬	Oxygen-rich blood
▬	Oxygen-poor blood

❷
Protective outer coat

Elastic and connective tissue

Muscle and elastic fibers

Inner lining

❸
Capillary wall

❹
Outer layer

Valve

Muscle layer

Inner lining

❷ ARTERY

This cutaway view of an artery shows its thick wall with both muscular and elastic layers. Arteries carry blood away from the heart. By expanding and bouncing back after every heartbeat, their walls withstand the high pressure of blood pumped by the heart. The artery's slick lining, as in veins, reduces friction and allows blood to flow smoothly.

❸ CAPILLARY

Capillaries are no wider than a single red blood cell, yet they make up 98 percent of the total length of all blood vessels. Capillaries connect the arteries to veins, infiltrating tissues to supply individual cells with their needs. Just one cell thick, capillary walls are leaky, allowing oxygen and food to pass freely to the body's cells.

❹ VEIN

Responsible for returning blood back to the heart, veins have thinner, less muscular walls than arteries. That's because they do not have to withstand high blood pressure. However, because blood in veins is under low pressure, the "push" driving it toward the heart is weak. Many veins have valves to stop blood flowing backward, away from the heart.

Digital arteries
carry blood to
the fingers

Femoral vein
drains blood from
the thigh

Posterior tibial
vein drains blood
from the foot and
lower leg

Posterior tibial artery
supplies blood to the
foot and lower leg

Femoral artery
supplies blood
to the thigh

Digital veins
drain blood
from the fingers

❺ HEART

A system that circulates blood around the body could not work without a means of propulsion. This is provided by the heart. A hollow, muscular pump, the heart has two sides that work in tandem. One side receives oxygen-poor blood from the body and pumps it to the lungs to pick up oxygen. The other side receives oxygen-rich blood from the lungs, then pushes it around the body.

CIRCULATION

Every second of the day and night blood circulates around the body to service trillions of cells that are dependent on its supplies to work normally. This circulation of blood is powered by the heart and takes place along an extensive network of living tubes called blood vessels, which would wrap twice around Earth if stretched out. There are three types of blood vessels—arteries, veins, and capillaries. Arteries carry blood from the heart, and branch repeatedly into smaller and smaller vessels that themselves divide into capillaries. These tiny blood vessels carry blood past every tissue cell, before uniting to form the veins that return blood to the heart. Together, the heart, blood vessels, and blood make up the circulatory system.

HEART

This fist-sized powerhouse of the circulatory system lies between the two lungs. The heart consists of two linked pumps, one that gets blood to the lungs to pick up oxygen, while the other supplies blood to the rest of the body. Valves inside the heart ensure one-way blood flow and, as they close, produce the thumping sounds that can be heard using a stethoscope. Made from cardiac muscle, which never tires, the heart beats some 2.5 billion times in an average lifetime without a pause.

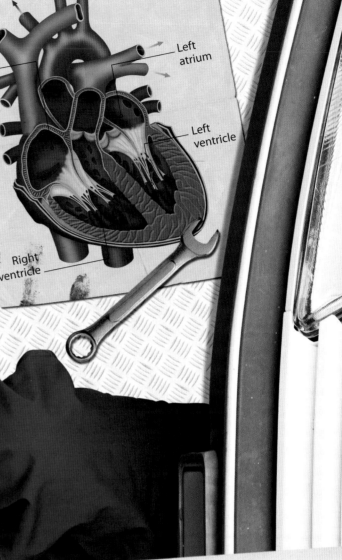

Right atrium

Left atrium

Left ventricle

Right ventricle

❶ HEART CHAMBERS
The heart is divided by a central wall into left and right halves. Each half of the heart has two chambers, a smaller, upper atrium, and a bigger, thicker-walled ventricle. The right part of the heart receives oxygen-poor blood from the body and pumps it to the lungs to pick up oxygen. The left side receives oxygen-rich blood from the lungs and pumps it to the body.

❷ HEARTBEAT STAGES
Each heartbeat is not one event but a sequence of stages that flow into each other, called atrial systole, ventricular systole, and diastole. This sequence is controlled by a natural pacemaker that is located in the wall of the right atrium. The pacemaker sends out electrical signals that make the walls of the atria contract first, followed just afterwards by the walls of the ventricles. Aided by valves that close to prevent backflow, this ensures that blood flows in only one direction—into then out of the heart.

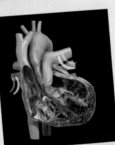

During atrial systole, the atria contract together to pump blood into the ventricles, opening the valves between upper and lower chambers.

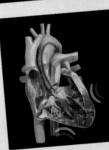

Contraction of the ventricles during ventricular systole forces blood out of the heart, closing valves between atria and ventricles to stop backflow.

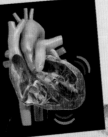

Heart muscle relaxes during diastole, allowing blood to enter the atria. Valves guarding exits from the ventricles close to prevent backflow.

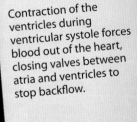

➍ BLOOD VESSELS

The heart is served by several major blood vessels. Those that transport oxygen-poor blood are shown in blue, those that carry oxygen-rich blood are shown in red. The right atrium receives blood from the superior vena cava and the inferior vena cava. The left atrium is supplied by a pair of pulmonary veins from each lung. The left ventricle exports blood along the aorta, while the pulmonary arteries carry blood from the right ventricle to both lungs.

Superior vena cava carries oxygen-poor blood from the head and upper body

Aorta carries oxygen-rich blood to the organs

Pulmonary artery carries oxygen-poor blood to the lungs

Pulmonary veins carry oxygen-rich blood from the lungs to the heart

➌ CHANGING HEART RATE

A seated person has a heart rate of around 70 beats per minute, but that will change according to the body's demands. If, for example, you go running, your muscles need much more oxygen and fuel, so heart rate increases to meet that demand. Heart rate is controlled by the body's autopilot, the autonomic nervous system (ANS), under orders from the brain stem. When you are active, the ANS instructs the pacemaker to speed up heart rate, and when you rest, the ANS tells it to slow down.

➎ HEART'S BLOOD SUPPLY

Hard-working heart muscles cannot obtain oxygen and food from the blood gushing through the heart's chambers. Instead, they receive supplies from two coronary arteries that arise from the aorta. These vessels carry oxygen and fuel to cardiac muscle cells to ensure that they continue contracting without tiring or taking a break.

LUNGS

Without oxygen there would be no life. Every body cell needs an uninterrupted supply of oxygen to "burn" the fuels that supply it with energy. We get oxygen supplies from the air. The act of breathing pulls air into two large organs, the lungs, that are enclosed inside the chest. Inside the lungs, oxygen passes continuously into the bloodstream to be carried to trillions of very demanding cells. The lungs, together with the air passages that link them to the outside world, make up the respiratory system.

❶ RESPIRATORY SYSTEM

The two nostrils, which lead to the nasal cavity, mark the entrance to the respiratory system. Confined to the head, neck, and chest, this system consists of the two lungs and the air passages—the nasal cavity, throat, larynx, trachea, and bronchi—that convey air to and from them. The lungs themselves are pinky-red, because of their rich blood supply, and spongy, because they are filled with air passages and sacs.

❷ NASAL CAVITY

Linking the nostrils to the throat, the nasal cavity processes breathed-in air to remove airborne dust and pathogens that would irritate the lungs. Once nostril hairs have trapped larger particles, air swirls around the nasal cavity depositing dirt and germs in the sticky mucus covering its lining. Contaminated mucus is then moved by hairlike cilia to the throat and swallowed. Air is also warmed and moistened here, making it even more acceptable to the lungs.

❸ TRACHEA

Running vertically behind the breastbone, the trachea, or windpipe, carries air to and from the lungs. At its lower end, it branches to form two primary, or main, bronchi that enter the lungs. The trachea's wall is reinforced with C-shaped rings of cartilage that stop it from collapsing inwards when air pressure drops as we breathe in. The lining of the trachea is moist with sticky mucus that traps dust and pathogens.

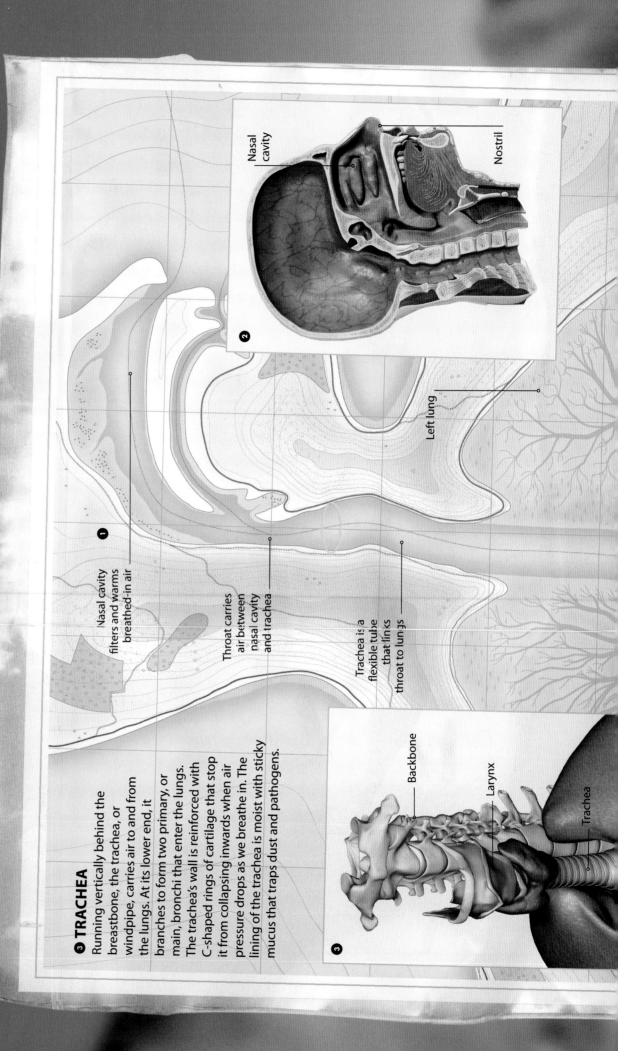

Nasal cavity filters and warms breathed-in air

Throat carries air between nasal cavity and trachea

Trachea is a flexible tube that links throat to lungs

Nasal cavity

Nostril

Left lung

Backbone

Larynx

Trachea

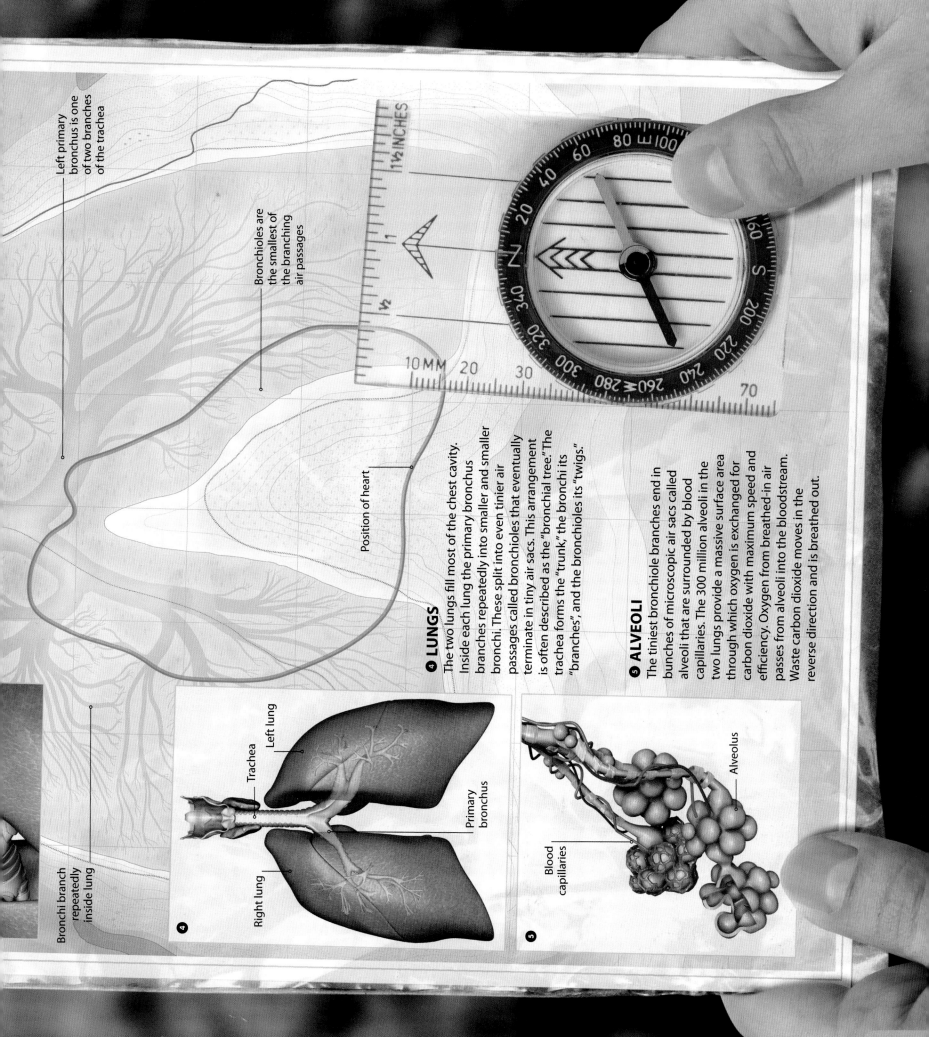

Left primary bronchus is one of two branches of the trachea

Bronchioles are the smallest of the branching air passages

1½ INCHES

10 MM 20 30 70

Position of heart

❹ LUNGS

The two lungs fill most of the chest cavity. Inside each lung the primary bronchus branches repeatedly into smaller and smaller bronchi. These split into even tinier air passages called bronchioles that eventually terminate in tiny air sacs. This arrangement is often described as the "bronchial tree." The trachea forms the "trunk," the bronchi its "branches", and the bronchioles its "twigs."

❺ ALVEOLI

The tiniest bronchiole branches end in bunches of microscopic air sacs called alveoli that are surrounded by blood capillaries. The 300 million alveoli in the two lungs provide a massive surface area through which oxygen is exchanged for carbon dioxide with maximum speed and efficiency. Oxygen from breathed-in air passes from alveoli into the bloodstream. Waste carbon dioxide moves in the reverse direction and is breathed out.

Bronchi branch repeatedly inside lung

Trachea

Left lung

Right lung

Primary bronchus

❹

Blood capillaries

Alveolus

❺

ENERGY

Put simply, energy is the capacity to do work. Without energy, cells cannot carry out the chemical reactions that keep us alive. Energy is stored in substances, such as carbohydrates, that we obtain from food. These fuels are broken down inside cells by a process called aerobic respiration. This uses the oxygen we breathe in to release stored energy. As well as providing the energy to make cells work, aerobic respiration also releases heat energy, which keeps us warm, and, in muscle cells, kinetic energy, which is used to move the body.

❶ EATING

Food provides us with energy. Our main food sources of energy are carbohydrates, including starch and sugars. During digestion, starch is broken down to the sugar glucose. This is absorbed into the bloodstream, and is our main "fuel." It is important to eat a balanced diet that includes a mixture of foods and also the right amount of energy. If someone takes in more energy than they need, they will store the excess as fat and put on weight.

❷ BREATHING

Although we can go for hours without eating or drinking, we cannot take a break from breathing. Even if someone holds their breath, the brain stem's respiratory center soon kicks in to restart breathing. Breathing ensures that an uninterrupted supply of oxygen enters the bloodstream, and that waste carbon dioxide is expelled. Our lungs evolved to work in air and cannot pick up oxygen underwater. That is why scuba divers carry an air supply.

❸ GAS EXCHANGE

In the lungs, oxygen passes from tiny baglike alveoli into the bloodstream in exchange for carbon dioxide. Gas exchange also occurs, as shown here, in all tissues from the brain to the big toe. As narrow capillaries carry blood through the tissues, oxygen leaves red blood cells and passes across the capillary wall to enter tissue cells. Carbon dioxide passes out of tissue cells, across the capillary wall, and into blood plasma to be carried away.

❹ CHANGING DEMANDS

During exercise, muscles need lots more energy and extra oxygen. If muscles do not get enough oxygen, they switch to a different type of respiration, which releases energy without using oxygen. This is called anaerobic respiration. However, the waste product of anaerobic respiration, lactic acid, must be removed. The amount of oxygen needed to do this is called the "oxygen debt," and rapid breathing helps to clear it.

❺ MITOCHONDRIA

This microscopic mitochondrion is the site of energy release inside all body cells. The breakdown of fuels, particularly glucose, begins in the cell's cytoplasm. It is inside mitochondria, however, that, with the help of oxygen, glucose molecules are dismantled to unlock their energy. This process is called aerobic respiration. Released energy is transferred to a carrier called ATP, which stores the energy until it is required by the cell.

❻ WASTE PRODUCTS

Each glucose molecule is constructed from six carbon, 12 hydrogen, and six oxygen atoms. During aerobic respiration, the carbon and oxygen atoms are released in the form of carbon dioxide, which passes into the bloodstream. This waste would be poisonous if allowed to remain in the body, so it is breathed out. Hydrogen atoms are combined with breathed-in oxygen to form water. Excess water can also be breathed out.

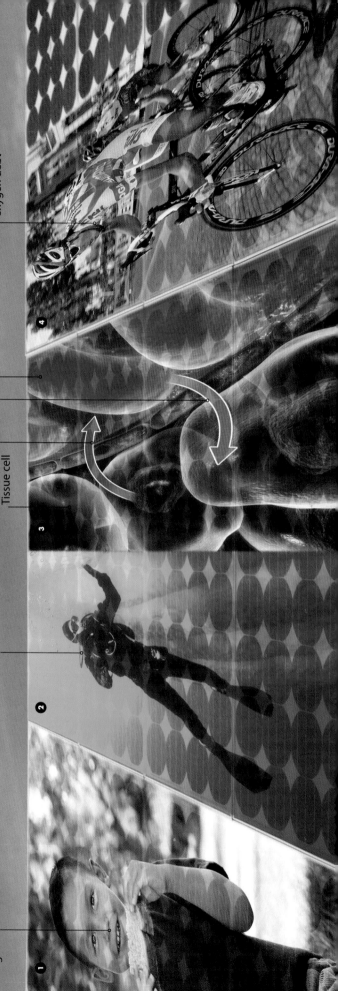

Red blood cell carries oxygen

Oxygen enters tissue cells

Waste carbon dioxide leaves tissue cells

Tissue cell

Panting after vigorous exercise cancels the oxygen debt

Humans need to carry oxygen in air tanks in order to breath underwater

The mouth is the starting point in the process of digesting food and absorbing fuel

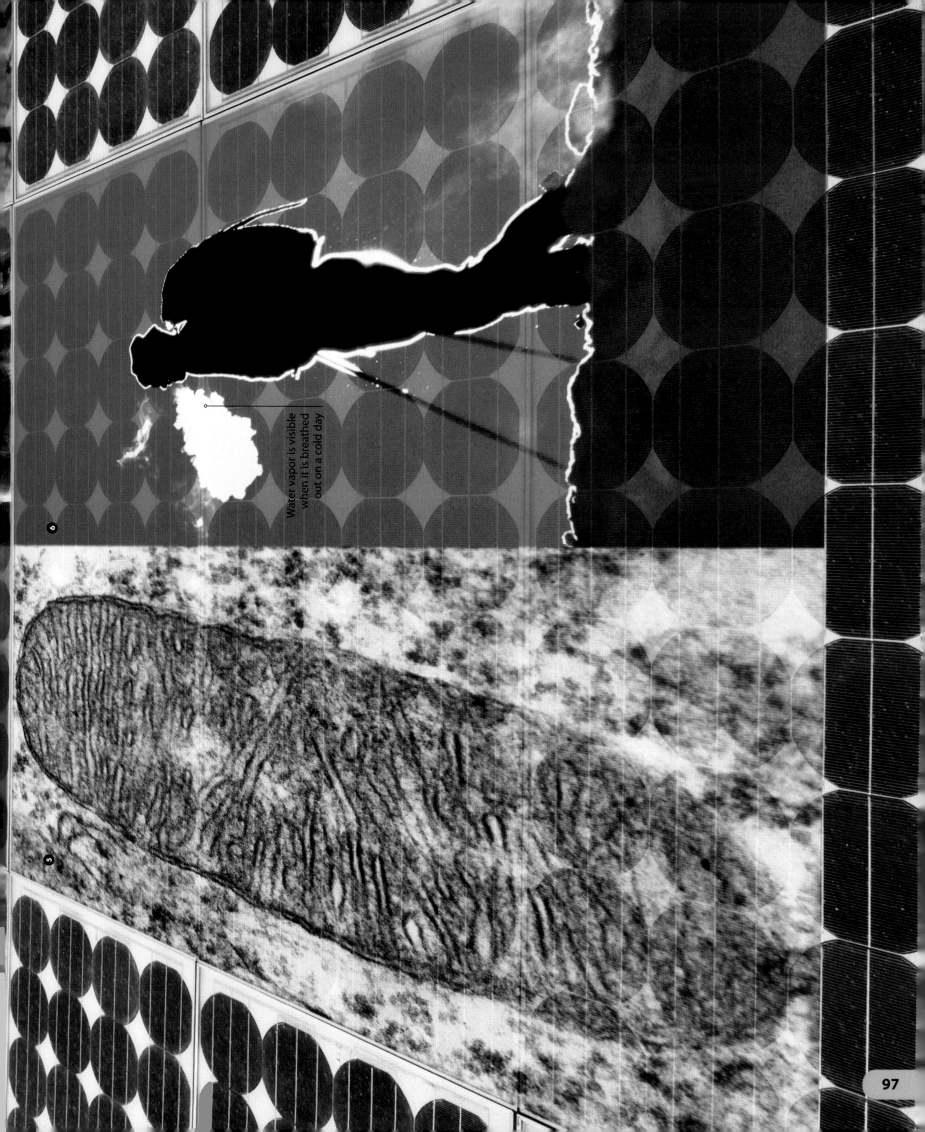

Water vapor is visible when it is breathed out on a cold day

BREATHING

Oxygen flows constantly from the lungs into the bloodstream to keep us alive. Waste carbon dioxide moves in the opposite direction. To maintain this flow, air in the lungs must be refreshed, with fresh, oxygen-rich air being brought in and stale, carbon dioxide-carrying air being removed. This is achieved by breathing or ventilation. Since the lungs cannot expand or shrink of their own accord, breathing is made possible by the diaphragm and rib muscles. Their actions make lungs act like bellows, to suck in and blow out air.

▶ INHALATION

During inhalation, or breathing in, the diaphragm, the domed sheet of muscle under the lungs, contracts, flattens, and pulls downward. At the same time, external intercostal muscles, which extend from rib to rib, contract, pulling the ribcage upward and outward. Together, these increase the space inside the chest. The elastic lungs follow these movements, expanding and sucking in air from the outside through the trachea.

Neck muscle pulls collarbone up to enlarge chest

Chest muscle helps to lift ribs

External intercostal muscles pull ribs upward and outward

Lungs expand as diaphragm pulls down and ribs pull out

Lungs shrink as the space inside the chest decreases

Diaphragm relaxes and is pushed upward into a dome shape

Internal intercostal muscles pull ribs downward during forced breathing

Diaphragm contracts, flattens, and pulls the lungs down

External intercostal muscles relax, allowing ribs to move downward and inward

◀ EXHALATION

Breathing out, or exhalation, is usually more passive than inhalation. As the diaphragm relaxes and is pushed upward, the external intercostal muscles relax so that the rib cage sinks downward and inward. These movements decrease the space inside the chest, and the elastic lungs shrink as air is squeezed out of them into the trachea. During exercise and other activities, the internal intercostals contract to actively pull the ribcage downward and force extra air out of the lungs.

◄ CONTROLLING BREATHING

How fast and deeply we breathe is controlled by the respiratory center in the brain stem. This is constantly updated by signals from receptors that detect levels of carbon dioxide or oxygen in the blood, or that monitor how stretched and hard-working muscles and tendons are. It sends signals to the diaphragm and intercostal muscles to alter the rate and depth of breathing to match our level of activity.

Brain stem

► BREATHING RATES

Under normal conditions, when we're not particularly active, we breathe in and out between 12 and 15 times every minute. During exercise, our skeletal muscles work harder, using up much more oxygen to liberate the energy they need to contract. At the same time, they release extra carbon dioxide into the blood. Both the rate and depth of breathing automatically increase to get more oxygen into the bloodstream and to eliminate excess carbon dioxide.

Coughing forces air from the lungs through the air passages and out of the mouth

► COUGHING AND SNEEZING

In addition to normal breathing, reflex movements, such as coughing and sneezing, help protect us. Both blow dust, obstructions, mucus, and other irritants out of the airways. During coughing, a deep breath is taken, the vocal cords are closed so that pressure builds up in the lungs, and then opened so that a blast of air removes irritants from the trachea and throat. Sneezing is similar, except that the air is forced out through the nose.

SPEAKING

Only humans have the ability to communicate with each other, using spoken language to pass on thoughts, instructions, emotions, and many other things. From the simple sounds we make as babies, we gradually learn to create words and phrases and to connect them together in sentences. Speaking is a highly sophisticated operation that is controlled by the brain. It also involves the respiratory system, to create a stream of air, the larynx, vocal cords, and the mouth.

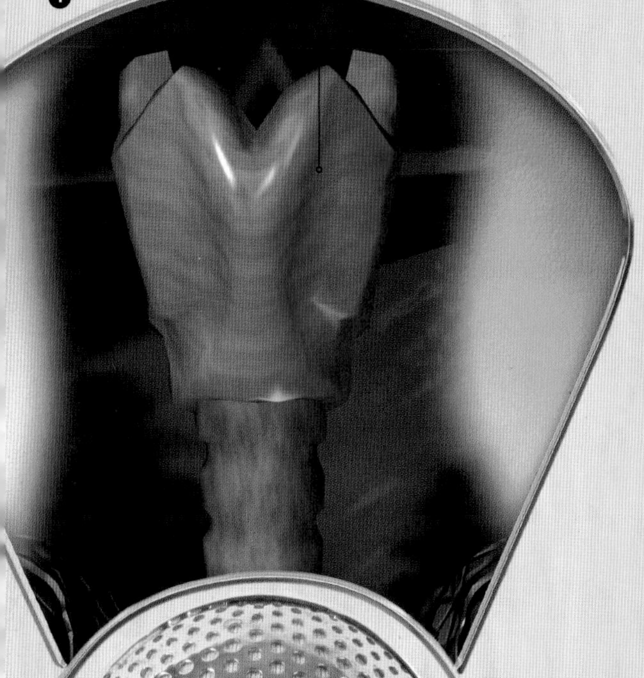

❶ LARYNX

Also called the voice box, the larynx connects the throat to the trachea. It is made from several plates of cartilage, one of which can be felt at the front of the neck as the "Adam's apple." These cartilages are held in place by ligaments and by muscles, some of which play a part in voice production. The two vocal cords stretch across the larynx from front to back.

❷ VOCAL CORDS

This photograph, taken using an endoscope, shows the view down a person's throat and into the larynx. Clearly visible are the vocal cords, ligaments that are made mainly of elastic fibers and are covered by membranes. The vocal cords are in a resting V-shaped position during normal breathing, when they are wide open and no sounds are being produced. The gap between them, called the glottis, allows the free passage of air to and from the lungs along the trachea, seen here disappearing downward below the larynx.

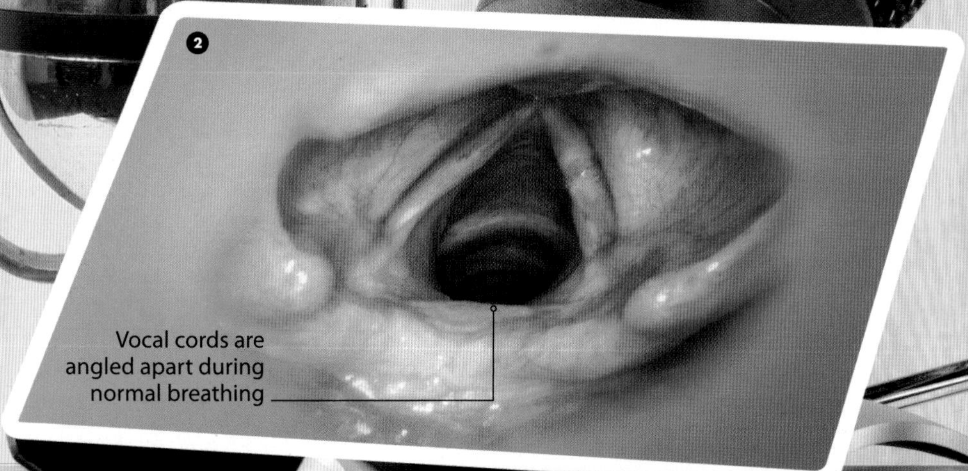

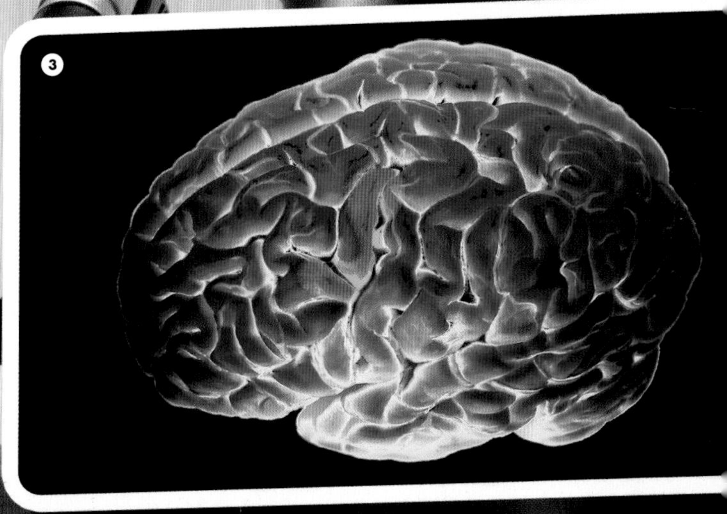

Vocal cords are angled apart during normal breathing

❸ BROCA'S AREA

Speech production is controlled by Broca's area in the left-hand side of the cerebral cortex. This scan shows Broca's area (red) in action. When a person chooses to speak, Broca's area sends signals to the adjacent motor areas of the cortex. These areas control muscles that alter breathing and pull the vocal cords together to create sounds, and also muscles in the lips and tongue that shape those sounds into speech.

❹ VIBRATING CORDS

Under instructions from the brain, larynx muscles pull the vocal cords together, to close or partially close the glottis, and make them taut. Controlled bursts of air from the lungs pass between the closed vocal cords and make them vibrate. These vibrations create buzzing sounds that require further processing to turn them into speech. If someone is talking or singing at length, larynx muscles relax periodically to open the glottis so that a person can take a breath.

❺ FORMING SOUNDS

The basic sounds generated by the vibrating vocal cords are improved and shaped in order that a person can speak words that are recognized by others. The throat acts rather like an organ pipe to amplify the sounds, while the mouth and nasal cavity make them more resonant. Through the process of articulation, muscles controlling the tongue, cheeks, and lips shape sounds into recognizable vowels and consonants.

Women have higher-pitched voices than men

Vocal cords are pulled together to make sounds

❻ HIGH AND LOW PITCH

The tenser the vocal cords are, the closer they are, and the faster they vibrate, the higher the pitch of the sounds produced by the vocal cords. Men have longer, thicker vocal cords than women, and because those vocal cords vibrate more slowly, men tend to have lower-pitched voices than women. The loudness of someone's voice depends on the force with which air passes between the vocal cords—a little force for a whisper and a large force for a shout.

FOOD

We eat food to get the nutrients that supply us with energy and the raw materials our bodies need for maintenance. Some nutrients we need in larger amounts, such as carbohydrates and fats for energy, and proteins for building materials. Vitamins and minerals are only needed in tiny amounts, but they are still essential. A balanced diet includes the right amounts and variety of foods and nutrients, as shown on this plate.

❶ FRUIT AND VEGETABLES

Apples, mangoes, and other fruits contain water and vitamins, as well as sugars (simple carbohydrates) that provide a quick burst of energy. They also supply dietary fiber that we do not digest, but which makes our intestines work more efficiently. Vegetables, such as peppers and broccoli, are rich in vitamins and minerals, and also contain fiber. Brightly colored fruit and vegetables also contain antioxidants that help protect us from heart disease, cancers, and other illnesses. That is why we should eat at least five portions of fruit and vegetables every single day.

❷ STARCHY FOODS

Foods such as rice, potatoes, and pasta are rich in starch. This complex carbohydrate is made of chains of sugar molecules, in this case glucose. During digestion, starch is gradually broken down in the small intestine into glucose, the body's main source of energy. Glucose is then absorbed into the bloodstream so it can be used by the body's cells. As well as being important energy sources, starchy foods also provide fiber, and supply the body with iron, calcium, and some B vitamins.

❸ WATER

This clear liquid does not supply you with energy or any building materials. Yet it is essential for life. Water makes up more than 50 percent of your body weight. It makes blood liquid and forms a big part of your cells' cytoplasm, the jellylike material in which the chemical reactions that keep you alive take place. You get water from not just drinks but almost all foods, even dry ones.

Carrots are a rich source of vitamin A

Bread contains lots of energy-rich starch

Water is constantly lost by the body and needs replacing

❹ FISH, MEAT, AND EGGS

Meat, fish, shellfish, and eggs are all good sources of protein, as are nuts and tofu for vegetarians. It is recommended that red meat is eaten in moderation because it also contains saturated fat—a food that if eaten in excess can be harmful for health. However, oily fish, such as salmon, is rich in omega-3 (unsaturated) fatty acids that are beneficial to health. During digestion, proteins are broken down into amino acids that the body uses to build its own proteins.

Fish is packed with protein

❺ SWEETS AND FATS

These may be the most attractive food items on the plate, but they are best eaten occasionally and in small amounts. Both sweet and fatty foods are laden with calories. If eaten to excess and too often, the extra energy they supply may be surplus to requirements. It is then stored as fat, making a person put on weight.

❻ DAIRY PRODUCTS

Produced by cows, buffaloes, sheep, and goats, milk and other dairy products, such as cheese, butter, and yogurt, are rich sources of the mineral calcium. This is essential for healthy teeth and bones, and for other body activities, such as muscle contraction. Some also supply protein, although dairy products, such as butter and certain cheeses, are also high in saturated fat and should be eaten in small amounts. In some parts of the world, especially in Africa and Asia, many people are intolerant of dairy products and cannot eat them.

Sweets are made from refined sugar

Cheese is an excellent source of calcium

MOUTH

Unlike hungry pythons, we cannot open our mouths wide to swallow our food whole. Instead, as the first part of the digestive system, the mouth processes food so it can be swallowed. The teeth bite food into chunks, slice it, then chew and crush it into small particles. The salivary glands douse food in saliva to aid the chewing process, assisted by the muscular tongue, which moves and mixes chewed particles. Now ready for the next part of digestion, food is swallowed into the stomach.

❶ TEETH TYPES

We have two sets of teeth in our lifetime. The first set of 20 milk teeth is replaced gradually during childhood by 32 permanent teeth, of which there are four types. Starting at the front, eight chisel-like incisors slice food into chunks, four pointed canines grip and tear food, and eight premolars and 12 molars, all equipped with broad crowns, grind and crush food into a paste.

❷ TOOTH STRUCTURE

The tooth's white working surface, the crown, is formed from enamel, the body's hardest material. It sits on a framework of bonelike dentine that extends downward to form the root. This is firmly anchored into a socket in the jaw bone, and the gums form a tight collar that stops bacteria reaching the root. A central pulp cavity contains blood vessels and nerves.

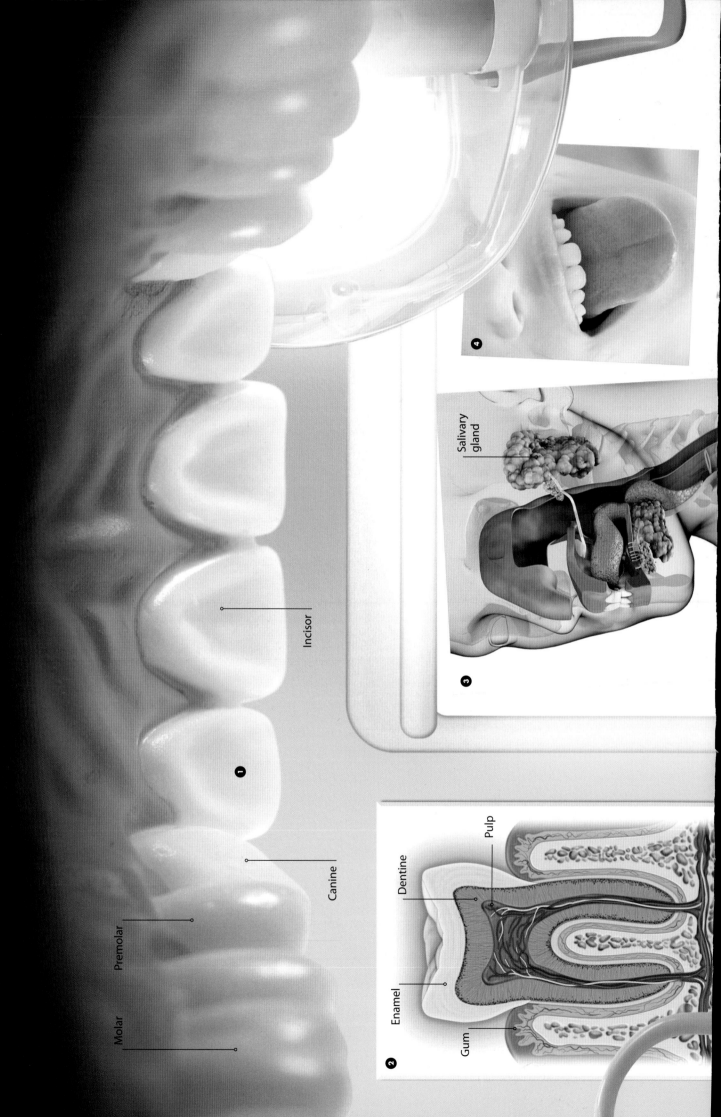

Molar

Premolar

Canine

❶

Incisor

Enamel

Dentine

Pulp

Gum

❷

Salivary gland

❸

❹

Soft palate blocks entrance to nasal cavity

Food pushed into oesophagus

Epiglottis covers entrance to trachea

Tongue pushes food to back of mouth

Epiglottis is raised in its normal position

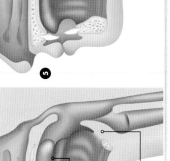

Temporalis

Masseter

③ SALIVARY GLANDS

Three pairs of salivary glands constantly release saliva into the mouth, helping to keep it moist and clean. If we are hungry, the sight, smell, or thought of food greatly increases saliva production in readiness for chewing. Mostly water, saliva also contains a starch-digesting enzyme and slimy mucus, which sticks chewed food particles together and lubricates food so that it is easier to swallow.

④ TONGUE

The tongue is equipped with a rough surface that grips food and continually moves it into position between the teeth for chewing. Thanks to careful coordination by the nervous system, it can do this without being bitten itself. The tongue also mixes food with saliva and forms it into a compact mass, ready for swallowing. Finally, the tongue's taste buds taste the food being eaten.

⑤ SWALLOWING

Once food has been thoroughly chewed, the tongue presses up and back to push the mass toward the throat. When food touches the back of the throat, it triggers an automatic reflex action. Throat muscles contract to move it into the oesophagus, the muscular tube that squeezes food to the stomach. At the same time, breathing stops briefly, and the opening to the trachea is blocked by the epiglottis to prevent choking.

⑥ JAW MUSCLES

Four pairs of jaw muscles power biting and chewing by lifting the lower jaw to bring the teeth together. The most powerful of these muscles are the temporalis and masseter. They pull the lower jaw upward to generate incredible pressure. The other jaw muscles produce the side to side movements of the jaw that grind food. In addition, cheek muscles keep food between the teeth during chewing.

DIGESTION

Hunger drives us to eat food several times a day to get hold of nutrients that supply us with energy and the raw materials for growth and repair. However, because nutrients are "locked up" inside food, it has to be broken down, or digested, to release them. That is the job of the digestive system. It breaks down food mechanically by crushing, grinding, or churning it. It also uses chemical digesters called enzymes to convert complex food molecules into simple nutrients, such as glucose, that can be absorbed into the bloodstream

❶ DIGESTIVE SYSTEM
The key part of the digestive system is a long tube, the alimentary canal, that runs down the middle of the body from mouth to anus. The different parts of the alimentary canal—the mouth, esophagus, stomach, small intestine, and colon (the main part of the large intestine)—work in sequence to process food efficiently in order to extract nutrients.

❷ MOUTH
When we eat, our front teeth bite into food and, aided by the lips, pull chunks into the mouth. As the tongue and cheeks move food between them, the back teeth crush it into a pulp. Saliva pours into the mouth to moisten the food particles. Once chewing is completed, the tongue molds food particles into a slimy ball, and this is pushed into the throat and swallowed.

❸ STOMACH
Linking the oesophagus to the small intestine, this J-shaped, expandable bag stores food to get digestion under way. Newly swallowed food is doused in highly acidic gastric juice that contains a protein-digesting enzyme, then churned by contractions of the stomach's muscular wall. The end result, after three to four hours, is a creamy liquid. This is released in small squirts through the pyloric sphincter, a ring of muscle that is usually tightly closed.

❹ PANCREAS
This long organ, shown here cut open, runs horizontally beneath the stomach and is connected to the duodenum, the first section of the small intestine. When part-digested food arrives from the stomach, the pancreas releases pancreatic juice into the duodenum. This juice contains enzymes that digest proteins, carbohydrates, and nucleic acids. Another enzyme digests fats, aided by bile, which is released by the gallbladder.

❺ LIVER
A big, busy organ, the liver has one direct role in digestion. It produces bile, which is stored in the gallbladder and released into the duodenum. Bile turns fats and oils into tiny droplets that are much more rapidly attacked by fat-digesting enzymes. Once digestion is completed, the liver processes food-rich blood, ensuring that vital nutrients are stored or dispatched to where they are needed.

❻ VILLI
Inside the small intestine, digestion is completed and its products are absorbed. Its lining is carpeted with millions of tiny, finger-like projections called villi that provide a massive surface for both digestion and absorption. Attached to the villi are enzymes that finish off digestion to release glucose, amino acids, and other simple nutrients. These nutrients are absorbed into blood capillaries inside the villi.

❼ FECES
Watery, indigestible waste is all that remains after digestion. As waste passes along the colon, it is dried out as water is taken back into the bloodstream. At the same time, trillions of colon bacteria feed on waste, color it brown, and release useful nutrients, such as vitamin K. The resulting lumps of waste, complete with their bacterial passengers, are called feces.

Esophagus carries food from mouth down to the stomach

Stomach

Large and small intestines

7

6

Blood capillaries
inside villus

3

Stomach has three
muscle layers

5

Gallbladder tucked
behind liver

Pyloric sphincter

Gallbladder
stores bile

4

Pancreatic duct
carries pancreatic
juice to duodenum

Opening of
pancreatic and bile
ducts into duodenum

LIVER

The body's second biggest organ after the skin, the liver plays a vital role in "cleaning up" the blood to help regulate its composition. Its cells, organized in processing units called lobules, carry out more than 500 functions. In relation to digestion, their only direct role is to produce bile, but they also store, convert, or break down nutrients arriving from the small intestine. The liver also contains white blood cells that remove bacteria and debris from the blood. The combined activities of liver cells release heat that helps to keep the body warm.

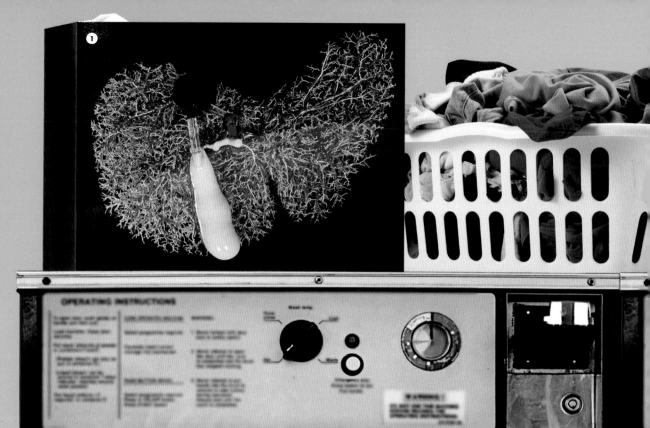

❶ BLOOD VESSELS
This image reveals the mass of blood vessels inside the liver. The liver is unusual in having two blood supplies. The hepatic portal vein (pale blue) carries oxygen-poor blood that is rich in nutrients from the small intestine, ready for processing by liver cells. The hepatic artery (red) delivers oxygen to liver cells. The yellow structure is the gallbladder that stores bile.

❷ LIVER CELLS
These hard-working cells carry out the many functions of the liver by processing blood as it flows past them. Liver cells deal with nutrients—including glucose, fats, and amino acids—absorbed from the small intestine in order to regulate their levels in the blood. They also store certain minerals and vitamins, make bile, break down hormones to stop them working, and remove poisonous substances from the blood.

❸ LIVER LOBULES

The liver's processing plants are its lobules, each no bigger than a sesame seed. A lobule contains vertical sheets of liver cells that radiate from a central vein. At the corners of lobules, branches of the hepatic vein deliver nutrient-rich blood, and branches of the hepatic artery deliver oxygen-rich blood. These mix and are processed by liver cells as they travel along wide capillaries to the central vein.

Central vein collects processed blood to be returned to the heart

Lobule contains radiating layers of liver cells

Branch of bile duct

Branch of hepatic artery delivers oxygen-rich blood

Branch of hepatic portal vein carries nutrient-rich blood

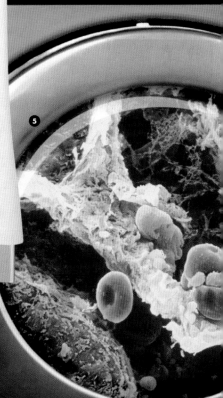

❹ BILE

This is the lining of the bile duct (green) that collects bile produced by liver cells and carries it for storage in the gallbladder and then to the small intestine. Bile is a yellow-green liquid that contains mainly water, but also bile salts, which help digest fats in the small intestine, and wastes, including the pigment bilirubin. Produced from the breakdown of hemoglobin from old red blood cells, bilirubin, once processed by gut bacteria, colors feces brown.

❺ KUPFFER CELLS

This highly magnified view inside a liver lobule captures activity inside a sinusoid, one of the large, leaky capillaries that passes between liver cells. The irregularly shaped yellow cell is a Kupffer cell, or hepatic macrophage. This is a type of white blood cell that lives permanently in the liver. It has trapped and is about to eat worn-out red blood cells, but it also removes bacteria and debris from the blood.

WASTE DISPOSAL

In order to work efficiently, it is vitally important for the body to maintain stable, unchanging conditions inside itself, especially in the bloodstream. The body's cells continually release potentially poisonous wastes into the blood. These poisons must not be allowed to accumulate and need to be disposed of. The urinary system plays a key role in maintaining stability by eliminating wastes and removing excess water and salts from the blood. Together, wastes, water, and salts are disposed of as urine.

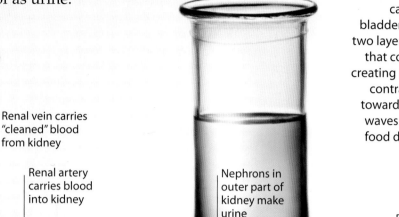

URETER ▼

Each of these hollow tubes arises from the hollow pelvis of the kidney, which receives a constant flow of urine from the nephrons. The ureters carry that urine to the bladder. Their walls contain two layers of smooth muscle that contract rhythmically, creating downward waves of contraction to push urine toward the bladder. Similar waves of contraction push food down the esophagus to the stomach.

Pelvis of kidney

Ureter connects kidney to bladder

Cross section through ureter shows muscle layer

Kidney filters blood to produce urine

Ureter carries urine from kidney to bladder

Renal vein carries "cleaned" blood from kidney

Renal artery carries blood into kidney

Pelvis of kidney channels urine into ureter

Nephrons in outer part of kidney make urine

Bladder stores urine, releasing it when convenient

Urethra carries urine to outside of the body

▲ URINARY SYSTEM

Two kidneys, two ureters, the bladder, and the urethra make up the urinary system. The kidneys filter blood that's received through the renal artery, to produce urine. Ureters carry urine to the bladder, where it is stored then released through the urethra. Each day, the kidneys process around 3,080 pints (1,750 liters) of blood to produce just 2.6 pints (1.5 liters) of urine.

▲ KIDNEYS

Shown here in cross section, each kidney has a darker-colored outer region that contains one million filtration units, called nephrons. Fluid containing both wastes, such as urea, and useful substances, such as glucose, is filtered from the blood into a tubular nephron. As the fluid passes along the nephron, useful substances pass back into the blood, while unwanted wastes, water, and salts form urine, which dribbles into the kidney's pelvis.

BLADDER ▼

This elastic bag expands from plum-sized to grapefruit-sized as it receives urine. The bladder's exit to the urethra is normally closed by ringlike sphincter muscles. When the bladder is full enough to make a person feel the need to urinate, the sphincter muscles relax, and smooth muscles in the bladder wall contract slowly and rhythmically to squeeze urine out of the body through the urethra.

▼ BLADDER CONTROL

Internal and external sphincter muscles guard the exit from the bladder. As the bladder expands, receptors in its wall send signals to the spinal cord, which tells the internal sphincter to relax. Messages sent to the brain make you feel the need to urinate and you can voluntarily relax your external sphincter to release urine. Babies and toddlers have to learn to control their external sphincter. That's why they have to wear diapers.

Bladder

Diapers are essential because babies cannot control release of urine

GERMS

Pathogens, or germs, are threats to our well-being. These are organisms that threaten to upset the normal workings of the body and cause disease or illness. Such pathogens range from the tiniest viruses, through single-celled bacteria to more complex protists, and beyond to fungi and bigger worms. What these organisms have in common is that they are all parasites, organisms that extract benefit from their host without giving anything back. They are also the cause of a range of serious illnesses that can affect a person's health.

▼ VIRUSES

These tiny, non-living packages consist of genetic instructions surrounded by a protective protein capsule. Once inside the body, viruses invade living cells in order to reproduce. They inject their genetic material and hijack the cell's normal metabolism to create multiple copies of new viruses that, once released, invade other body cells. This virus is HIV, which infects some of the body's immune cells, weakening the body's defences and causing a disease called AIDS.

Spikes (antigens) allow virus to attach to, or break out of, host cells

Capsule surrounds virus's genetic material

◀ FLU VIRUS

Viruses are identified by markers, or antigens, that project from their surfaces. This flu virus, for example, has two types of antigens. One type helps the virus attach to and invade cells in the upper part of the respiratory system. Those infected cells and the body's immune system respond by causing the inflammation, high temperature, and other symptoms that are typical of flu. The other type of antigen helps the newly formed viruses escape from their host body cells.

▶ BACTERIA

The most abundant life forms on Earth, bacteria are relatively simple, single-celled organisms. Some bacteria are pathogenic, including this *Vibrio cholerae*, which is picked up from contaminated water and causes the severe, sometimes fatal, diarrhea of cholera. Pathogenic bacteria trigger disease by attaching to body cells and releasing poisons called toxins. They cause diseases such as diphtheria, typhoid, and plague. Each bacteria reproduces by splitting into two separate bacteria.

Whiplike flagellum rotates to propel bacterium

◀ PROTISTS

These single-celled organisms, bigger than bacteria, include lots of free-living forms, such as amoeba, as well as some pathogens. Giardia (left), for example, is picked up from contaminated water and infects the intestines to cause severe diarrhea and sickness. Another protist, Plasmodium, is spread by mosquitoes and causes malaria. This tropical disease affects 500 million people, and kills over one million every year.

"Suction pad" attaches Giardia to intestinal lining

▶ FUNGI

Neither plants nor animals, some fungi are pathogens that grow in living tissues. This micrograph shows a fungus that feeds on skin flakes and causes ringworm, a disease that produces red circles on the skin. Its branching filaments or hyphae penetrate the skin and digest the host's cells. Similar fungi cause athlete's foot.

Hypha

Spores released from these structures enable fungus to spread

◀ ROUNDWORM

Like their name suggests, roundworms are cylindrical in shape. Some, such as hookworms and pinworms, are parasites in humans. Hookworms are picked up by walking barefoot on soil infected by their larvae. The larvae penetrate the skin, migrate to the lungs, are coughed up and swallowed, and arrive in the intestine. Adult hookworms live in the small intestine to which they are attached by the worm's hooklike "teeth." Hookworms cause diarrhea and pain as a result of their feeding on blood from the intestinal wall.

"Teeth" secure hookworm to host's intestine

▼ FLUKES

Relatives of flatworms found in streams, flukes are parasites, some causing disease in humans. Schistosomiasis is a tropical disease affecting 200 million people worldwide. It is picked up by swimming in water infested with fluke larvae, which burrow through the skin. Adult schistosome flukes grow in veins surrounding the intestines or bladder. The male fluke encloses the female (below), and her eggs are passed out in feces or urine. Those eggs also cause tissue damage and weaken the body.

▼ TAPEWORMS

Another parasitic relative of flatworms, tapeworms live in the intestines. Here, lacking a digestive system, they "soak up" nutrients. Each tapeworm consists of a headlike scolex and a ribbonlike body, up to 33 ft (10 m) long. Hooks and suckers on the scolex anchor the tapeworm to the intestinal lining. The body consists of segments that produce eggs, before detaching and leaving through the anus in feces to infect new hosts.

Ring of hooks secure tapeworm to its host

BARRIERS

The threat to the body of invasion by pathogens is relentless. Pathogens, including bacteria, viruses, and fungi, can arrive in the air, in food or drink, or through direct contact. As a first line of defence, the body employs basic barriers to stop pathogens before they can get into the tissues or bloodstream and cause infection. These include physical barriers, such as the skin and the epithelium that lines passageways in the body, as well as chemicals such as in tears and stomach juice. Any invaders that do break through are mopped up by white blood cells.

▼ SALIVA

Released continuously, saliva washes around the mouth, over the tongue, and around the teeth, helping to control bacteria and destroy pathogens that arrive in food and drink. Like tears, saliva contains antibodies that target pathogens, along with bacteria-killing lysozyme that, in the mouth, helps prevent tooth decay. Saliva also contains defensins, substances that kill bacteria in mouth cuts and summon white blood cells to tackle invaders.

◄ SKIN BACTERIA

Unless it is cut, your skin presents a strong barrier to bacteria and other pathogens. However, there is also a rather unlikely defence force on the skin's surface. This is *Acinetobacter baumanii*, one of the many types of bacteria that live on the skin. Together, these bacteria form the skin's "flora," a community of "friendly" microorganisms that between them prevent more harmful pathogens from settling and growing on the skin's surface.

◄ LINING CELLS

This cross section through the small intestine shows column-shaped epithelial cells (brownish with a pink nucleus) in its lining packed together, without any gaps, to form a barrier that stops pathogens getting into underlying tissues or into the bloodstream. Similar epithelial linings are found in the other parts of the digestive system, as well as in the respiratory, urinary, and reproductive systems. These linings may also produce sticky mucus that traps and disables pathogens.

▼ TEARS

With every blink, tears naturally wash over the front of the eyeball, removing any dirt or debris as they do so. At the same time, they moisten this exposed part of the eye and stop it from drying out—dry eyes are red and painful and can invite infection by bacteria or viruses. Tears also contain lysozyme, an enzyme that damages bacteria and kills them, along with antibodies that target and disable specific pathogens.

▶ STOMACH ACID

This microscopic view of the stomach's lining shows gastric pits, the openings to the glands that make and release gastric juice. A mix of enzymes and acid, gastric juice helps digest food. One of its key ingredients is hydrochloric acid, an acid that is so strong that, outside the body, it can strip paint. Inside the stomach, it makes conditions so harsh that few of the bacteria arriving in food and drink can survive.

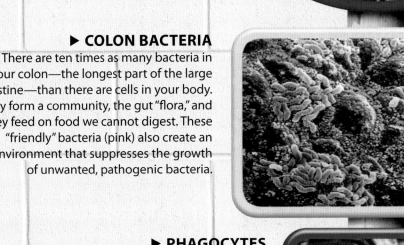

▶ COLON BACTERIA

There are ten times as many bacteria in your colon—the longest part of the large intestine—than there are cells in your body. They form a community, the gut "flora," and they feed on food we cannot digest. These "friendly" bacteria (pink) also create an environment that suppresses the growth of unwanted, pathogenic bacteria.

▶ PHAGOCYTES

The foot soldiers of the body's immune system, phagocytes are white blood cells that travel through blood, lymph, and body tissues in search of invading pathogens. This macrophage (pink), a type of phagocyte, has tracked down bacteria (yellow) that it is about to engulf and destroy.

▶ MUCUS

The air we breathe carries particles of dust, pollen grains, bacteria, and viruses that would harm the lungs. To prevent that occurring, the lining of the nasal cavity, trachea (right), and other parts of the respiratory system secrete sticky mucus. As breathed-in air swirls around, it deposits particles and pathogens into the mucus where they become stuck. Then tiny cilia move the dirty mucus to the throat, where it is swallowed and dealt with by the stomach (see above).

LYMPH

Like the circulatory system, the lymph or lymphatic system has vital roles in transport and defence. Its vessels drain surplus fluid, called lymph, from body tissues and return it to the bloodstream in order to restore normal blood volume. Without this service, our tissues would swell up. The lymph system's lymphoid organs contain white blood cells, called lymphocytes and macrophages, that play a key part in the body's immune system. These cells remove pathogens carried in lymph, by the blood, or in the air.

● LYMPH SYSTEM

This consists of a network of vessels and lymphoid organs, including lymph nodes, tonsils, and the spleen. The smallest vessels, lymph capillaries, merge to form larger lymph vessels. The largest of these join two main ducts that empty lymph into the bloodstream in the subclavian veins. A one-way flow of lymph is maintained along vessels by surrounding skeletal muscles, which squeeze vessels when they contract, and by valves, like those found in veins.

Tonsils trap pathogens in food or air

Left subclavian vein receives lymph

Spleen is the largest lymphoid organ

Lymph vessels end in dead-end capillaries

Lymph node filters lymph passing through it

● LYMPH CAPILLARIES

As blood flows through tissues, fluid leaks from blood capillaries and carries oxygen and food to tissue cells. Most of that fluid returns to blood capillaries, but some remains. This surplus is collected by a branching network of blind-ending lymph capillaries that pass, just like blood capillaries, between tissue cells. Lymph capillaries have tiny flaps in their walls that allow excess tissue fluid into them, but not out again. This clear fluid, now called lymph, passes from lymph capillaries into larger lymph vessels.

Blood capillaries carry blood between tissue cells

Blind-ending lymph capillaries collect excess fluid

116

❸ LYMPH NODES

The most numerous lymphoid organs, these small swellings, each protected by a tough capsule, occur along lymph vessels. As lymph flows through lymph nodes, it is filtered. Spaces inside the node contain networks of fibers that support macrophages, which eat bacteria and debris, and lymphocytes, which detect pathogens and launch a response. When fighting an infection, lymph nodes may swell and become tender, a condition known as "swollen glands."

❹ LYMPHOCYTES

These lymphocytes (yellow) are the stalwarts of the immune system. A type of white blood cell, lymphocytes are found in vast numbers in lymph nodes and other lymphoid organs where they intercept pathogens. There are two main types of lymphocyte. T lymphocytes directly attack body cells infected with pathogens, such as viruses. B lymphocytes release antibodies, chemicals that cripple bacteria and highlight them for destruction.

❺ SPLEEN

The biggest lymphoid organ, the spleen has a rich blood supply and is located to the left of the stomach. The spleen provides a site where lymphocytes can detect and destroy pathogens, and where they can multiply to launch an even stronger immune response should the body become infected. It also contains macrophages that "clean" the blood by engulfing bacteria and worn-out red blood cells.

❻ TONSILS

Five tonsils—two at the back of the mouth (shown here), two at the base of the tongue, and one near the exit from the nasal cavity—guard the throat, the entrance to the digestive and respiratory systems. Bacteria carried on food and in the air enter the tonsils, get trapped, and are destroyed by lymphocytes. Tonsils grow to full size during childhood, when they often get infected.

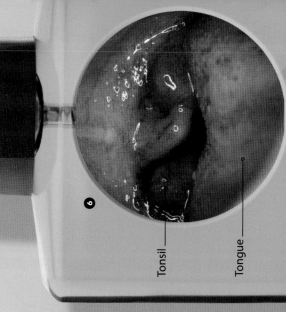

Tonsil

Tongue

Fiber network supports lymphocytes and macrophages

Incoming lymph vessel delivers lymph into node

Germinal centre where lymphocytes multiply

Single lymph vessel carries lymph away from node

T LYMPHOCYTES

T cells, or T lymphocytes, patrol the body and destroy invaders, such as viruses that infect body cells. There are three types of T cells—helper T cells, killer T cells, and memory T cells. An inactive killer T cell becomes activated when it identifies and matches the antigens of a specific pathogen. When the same antigen is recognized by a helper T cell, it stimulates the activated killer T cell to divide rapidly to produce masses of clones that destroy infected cells directly. The helper T cells and killer T cells also produce memory T cells that "remember" the invader for future reference.

KILLER T CELLS

Killer T cells (also called cytotoxic T cells) are the only lymphocytes that directly destroy other cells. Once activated by helper T cells, they travel in blood and lymph, attacking both body cells infected by viruses and cancer cells. The killer T cell identifies its target cell through markers on the diseased cell's outer membrane. Here, killer T cells (orange) launch a chemical attack on a cancer cell (pink), causing it to disintegrate.

DEFENDERS

The most sophisticated and powerful part of the body's immune or defence system centers on white blood cells called lymphocytes. Found particularly in the lymphatic system, lymphocytes identify pathogens by their antigens, markers carried on their surfaces that identify them as foreign. There are two basic types of lymphocyte—T and B—that use different strategies to kill pathogens. Whatever the type, however, each lymphocyte only responds to one specific pathogen, and also retains a memory of its enemy. If it invades again, it is quickly destroyed, giving us immunity to that disease.

B LYMPHOCYTES

This division of the immune army, also called B cells, targets mainly bacteria. B cells work by releasing disabling chemicals called antibodies. Each B cell responds to a specific pathogen, recognizing the antigens that make it different from a body cell. If receptors on the surface of a B cell match the antigens on an invading pathogen, it becomes activated. Stimulated by helper T cells, the B cell divides rapidly to produce big plasma cells that pour out the antibodies that target the invader. Also produced are long-lived memory B cells that "remember" and respond to the pathogen in case it invades again.

ANTIBODIES

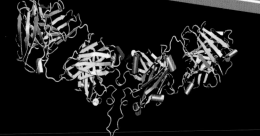

This computer model shows a Y-shaped antibody molecule. Antibodies are proteins released into blood and lymph by B cells when pathogens invade the body. Each type of antibody acts against a specific pathogen, as identified by its surface antigens. The arms of the "Y" differ in structure from one antibody type to the next, because that's the part that binds to the particular shape of antigen. When antibodies stick to a pathogen, they disable it and mark it for destruction by phagocytes, or by other blood proteins.

PHAGOCYTOSIS

Here, a white blood cell is surrounding and about to eat pathogenic bacteria (red). This process is called phagocytosis. As well as destroying pathogens, many of these white cells, including macrophages, have another role. Having eaten their prey, they display some of its antigens on their surface. They then "present" the antigens to helper T cells, and these release chemicals called cytokines that can activate both B cells and killer T cells.

IMMUNIZATION

The first time we are infected by a pathogen, it takes days for the immune system to launch its antibody response. However, if the same pathogen returns we are resistant to infection because the immune system is primed for action. Unfortunately, some first-time pathogens cause serious infections before the immune system can take action. Immunization gives us resistance to such pathogens. Injecting a harmless version of the pathogen stimulates an immune response of the pathogen that gives us resistance without causing illness.

TREATMENT

There are many different types of disease, but they all have something in common—they disrupt the normal working of the body. Infectious diseases, such as measles, are caused by pathogens. Non-infectious diseases, such as heart attacks or cancers, are triggered by genes or lifestyle. Thanks to advances in modern medicine, there are many possible treatments for this array of illnesses and conditions.

▼ DIAGNOSIS

To treat disease, a doctor first works out what is wrong with a patient by making a diagnosis. This involves asking about symptoms—what the patient has noticed. The doctor will then look for signs of disease by examining the patient and by conducting tests, such as measuring blood pressure with a sphygmomanometer (below).

◀ FIRST AID

This is the initial help and care given to a person to treat an illness or injury before, if necessary, medical treatment can be given. First-aiders are given training in techniques to deal with anything from a simple cut to life-threatening situations such as choking. Many homes are equipped with a simple first-aid kit (left), containing bandages and other basics.

▶ DRUGS

Once doctors have diagnosed a disease, they may decide to use a drug to treat it. Drugs are chemicals that treat disease by changing how the body works, or by destroying the pathogens that are causing the disease. Examples of the many different types of drugs include antibiotics, which kill bacteria, and analgesics, which relieve pain. Drugs may be poisonous and should always be taken in doses recommended by a doctor.

◀ SURGERY

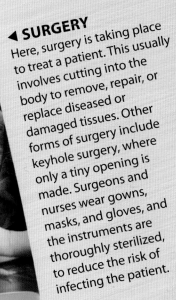

Here, surgery is taking place to treat a patient. This usually involves cutting into the body to remove, repair, or replace diseased or damaged tissues. Other forms of surgery include keyhole surgery, where only a tiny opening is made. Surgeons and nurses wear gowns, masks, and gloves, and the instruments are thoroughly sterilized, to reduce the risk of infecting the patient.

◀ RADIOTHERAPY

The term cancer describes a number of serious diseases, including lung cancer and colon cancer, that result from abnormal tissue cells dividing uncontrollably to produce growths called tumors. These stop the body functioning normally. Tumors can be treated using surgery or drugs, but also by radiotherapy. The patient's affected area is exposed to high-energy radiation that penetrates the tissues to kill cancerous cells.

▶ ALTERNATIVE THERAPIES

These are techniques that are used in addition to, or instead of, modern medicine in an attempt to treat various conditions. They include traditional medicine, herbalism, reflexology, osteopathy, aromatherapy, and, as shown here, acupuncture. This ancient Chinese treatment involves inserting the tips of fine needles into specific places in the skin to open "energy channels" with a resulting beneficial effect.

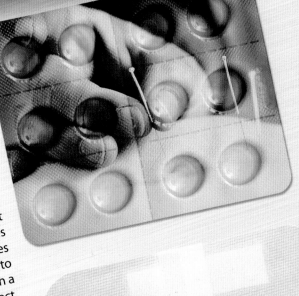

▶ PHYSIOTHERAPY

A trained physiotherapist uses various physical techniques to restore the normal workings of the body, or to improve mobility and flexibility, following illness, surgery, an accidental injury, or when someone is immobile for a long period. These techniques include exercise, massage, manipulation, and electrical stimulation. Here, a patient is being treated in a hydrotherapy pool. Being in water means that she is effectively weightless, so can exercise her upper body without putting any strain on her legs.

SPARE PARTS

During a lifetime, body parts become damaged through overuse, because of disease, or following an accident. In the past, a person would have to put up with such damage or might even die because of it. Today, however, modern medicine provides many solutions in the form of spare parts to fix these body malfunctions. For example, worn out joints can be rebuilt and replacement organs can be transplanted.

❶ REPLACEMENT JOINTS
Age and disease can damage bones and joints, but it is possible to repair such damage using replacement joints. This X ray of the hip shows an artificial joint between the femur (thigh bone) and pelvic girdle. The surgeon has replaced diseased bone with a prosthesis (blue) made of metal or plastic, the head of which fits into a new socket in the hip bone to form a replacement ball and socket joint. Other joints that can be replaced in a similar way include the knee and shoulder.

❷ ORGAN TRANSPLANTS
In an operating theatre, a surgeon opens a bag containing a kidney very recently removed from someone who donated the organ. The kidney will now be transplanted into a patient whose own kidneys have failed. Once connected to the patient's blood supply, the transplanted kidney will filter the blood to remove water and wastes. There is always a risk that the patient's immune system will attack and reject the "foreign" organ from the other person, so the patient has to take drugs to suppress any immune response. Many other organs can be transplanted, including the liver and heart.

❸ GROWING ORGANS

Transplanting an organ with a replacement from another person runs the risk that the recipient's body might reject the "foreign" organ. An alternative solution is to grow a new, "non-foreign" organ in the laboratory from a patient's own cells. This bladder (pink) was grown around a mold before being transplanted into a patient.

❹ STEM CELLS

These stem cells (pink and brown) are unspecialized, but have the ability to give rise to many types of specialized cells, such as nerve cells. It may be possible in the future to use stem cells to repair damaged or diseased tissue in patients. Stem cells would generate replacement cells to repair tissues.

❼ BIONIC LIMBS

Artificial limbs have been used for many years, but modern technology has now made it possible to develop thought-controlled bionic limbs. This woman has a bionic arm wired to her chest muscles. When she thinks about moving the arm, hand, or fingers, instructions travel from her brain to her chest muscles. These then send signals to a tiny computer that tells her arm precisely how to move.

❺ ARTIFICIAL PACEMAKER

The heart has a built-in, natural pacemaker that sets the rate at which it beats. In some people, this stops working properly and the heart beats too slowly or too irregularly. One solution is to use an artificial pacemaker. This X ray of the chest shows an artificial pacemaker, equipped with a long-life battery, implanted under the skin. It sends

❻ COCHLEAR IMPLANT

This surgically implanted device gives a sense of sound to people who would otherwise have little or no hearing because the inner parts of their ears do not function properly. An external microphone picks up sounds that are transmitted to an internal receiver, and this sends signals to the hearing part of the brain.

Glossary

ADOLESCENCE
The period of transition between childhood and adulthood that occurs during the teenage years.

AEROBIC RESPIRATION
The release of energy from glucose and other fuels that takes place inside cells and requires oxygen.

AMINO ACID
One of a group of 20 chemicals that are the building blocks from which proteins are made.

ANAEROBIC RESPIRATION
The release of energy from glucose and other fuels that takes place inside cells and does not require oxygen.

ANTIBODY
A type of protein released by immune system cells that disables pathogens, such as bacteria, and marks them for destruction.

ANTIGEN
A marker on the surface of bacteria and other pathogens that is recognized as "foreign" by the immune system.

AUTONOMIC NERVOUS SYSTEM (ANS)
The part of the nervous system that automatically controls many body processes such as heart rate and changing pupil size.

AXON
A nerve fiber—the long filament that extends from a neuron's cell body and carries signals to another neuron or a muscle.

BACTERIA
A group of microorganisms, some of which cause diseases such as cholera.

BILLION
A number equal to one thousand million (1,000,000,000).

BIONIC
Describes an artificial body part that is usually electrically operated.

CALCIUM
A mineral that is used by the body to help build teeth and bones.

CARBON DIOXIDE
A gas that is the waste product of energy release in cells and is breathed out into the air.

CARDIAC MUSCLE
A type of muscle found only in the heart.

CARTILAGE
A tough, flexible connective tissue that covers the ends of bones in joints and helps support the body.

CELL
One of the 100 trillion microscopic living units from which the body is built.

CENTRAL NERVOUS SYSTEM (CNS)
The control center of the nervous system that consists of the brain and the spinal cord.

CEREBRAL CORTEX
The thin surface layer of the brain's cerebrum that processes information relating to thought, memory, the senses, and movement.

CHROMOSOME
One of 46 threadlike structures in a cell's nucleus. Chromosomes are made of DNA and contain genes.

CILIA
Microscopic, hairlike projections from certain body cells that beat back and forth to move materials, such as mucus and dust, across their surface.

COLLAGEN
A tough, fibrous protein that gives strength to connective tissues such as cartilage.

CRANIUM
The upper, domed part of the skull that surrounds and protects the brain.

CYTOPLASM
The jellylike liquid that fills a cell between the cell membrane and nucleus.

DEOXYRIBONUCLEIC ACID (DNA)
One of the long molecules found in the nucleus that contains the coded instructions to build and operate a cell.

DIASTOLE
The part of the heartbeat sequence when the chambers of the heart are relaxed.

EMBRYO
The name given to a developing baby between the time it arrives in the uterus until eight weeks after fertilization.

ENDOSCOPE
A viewing instrument used to look inside the body.

ENERGY
The capacity to perform work. It is essential to keep a cell functioning.

ENZYME
A type of protein that acts as a biological catalyst. Enzymes greatly accelerate the rate of chemical reactions inside and outside cells, such as the breakdown of food as it passes through the intestines.

EVOLUTION
The process by which living things change over time and that gives rise to new species.

EXTENSOR
A skeletal muscle that increases the angle of a joint, such as straightening the arm at the elbow.

FETUS
The name given to a developing baby from the ninth week after fertilization until its birth.

FLEXOR
A skeletal muscle that decreases the angle of a joint such as bending the arm at the elbow.

FUNGI
A group of living organisms, including mushrooms and molds, some of which cause disease in humans.

GASTRIC
Describes something relating to the stomach.

GENE
One of the 23,000 instructions contained within the DNA in a cell's nucleus. Genes control the production of proteins that build and operate a cell.

GLAND
A group of cells that produce substances that are released into or onto the body.

GLUCOSE
A simple type of sugar that circulates in the bloodstream and is the main energy source for the body's cells.

HAIR FOLLICLE
A deep pit in the skin from which a hair grows.

HELPER T CELL
A type of white blood cell, called a lymphocyte, that activates other immune system cells.

HEPATIC
Describes something relating to the liver.

HOMININ
A member of a group that includes living and extinct human species, including modern humans (*Homo sapiens*) and *Homo erectus*.

HORMONE
A substance released by a gland into the bloodstream that acts a chemical messenger. Hormones control certain body processes including reproduction and the rate of body growth.

HUNTER-GATHERER
A member of a group of nomadic people who exist by hunting and collecting plant food, rather than through agriculture.

IMMUNE SYSTEM
A collection of cells in the circulatory and lymph systems that protect the body from pathogens and the diseases they can cause.

JOINT
A part of the skeleton where two or more bones meet.

KERATIN
A tough, waterproof protein found in hairs, nails, and the skin's epidermis.

LIGAMENT
One of the strong bands of connective tissue that hold bones together at joints.

LYMPH
The excess liquid that is drained from the tissues, carried along lymph vessels, then returned to the bloodstream.

LYMPHOCYTE
A type of white blood cell that plays a key part in the immune system.

LYMPHOID
Describes organs associated with the lymph system.

LYSOZYME
A type of protein, found in tears, saliva, and sweat, which kills certain harmful bacteria.

MACROPHAGE
A type of large white blood cell that engulfs and destroys pathogens and plays a part in the immune system.

MELANIN
A brown-black pigment that colors skin and hair.

METABOLIC RATE
The rate at which energy is released by metabolism, the sum total of all the chemical processes happening inside every one of the body's cells.

MICROGRAPH
A photograph taken with the aid of a microscope.

MICROORGANISM
A tiny living thing, such as a bacterium, that can only be seen using a microscope.

MILLION
A number equal to one thousand thousand (1,000,000).

MINERAL
One of more than 20 chemicals, including iron and calcium, that are needed for good health and must be present in the diet.

MITOCHONDRION
One of several structures in a cell's cytoplasm that release energy. The plural of mitochondrion is mitochondria.

MITOSIS
A type of cell division that produces two identical cells. Mitosis is used for body growth and to replace damaged or worn-out cells.

MOLECULE
A group of atoms that are bonded together, such as the carbon, hydrogen, and oxygen atoms that form a glucose molecule.

MOTOR NEURON
A type of neuron that carries nerve impulses from the central nervous system to muscles and glands around the body.

MUCUS
A thick, slimy fluid that protects and lubricates the linings of the respiratory and digestive systems.

MUSCLE
A type of tissue that contracts, or gets shorter, to produce movement.

NERVE IMPULSE
A tiny electrical signal that passes along a neuron at high speed, carrying information and instructions to parts of the body.

NEURON
One of the billions of interconnected nerve cells that make up the nervous system.

NOMADIC
Describes people who have no fixed home and travel from place to place.

NUCLEUS
The control center of a cell that contains its DNA.

NUTRIENT
A substance, such as a carbohydrate, protein, or fat, that is obtained from food and is essential for normal body functioning.

OLFACTORY
Describes something relating to the sense of smell.

ORGAN
A body part, such as the kidney, brain, or the stomach, that is made up of two or more types of tissue, and which has a specific role or roles.

ORGANISM
An individual living thing.

OXYGEN
A gas found in air that is breathed in, absorbed by the bloodstream, and used by cells to release energy from glucose.

PATHOGEN
Any type of microorganism, including bacteria, viruses, and protists, that cause disease.

PHAGOCYTE
A type of white blood cell that engulfs and destroys bacteria and debris.

PROTIST
One of a group of single-celled organisms, some of which cause diseases such as malaria.

PUBERTY
Part of adolescence when the body grows rapidly and develops an adult appearance, and when the reproductive system starts working.

RECEPTOR
A specialized nerve cell or the end of a neuron that detects a stimulus such as light, odor, sound, or touch.

REFLEX
A rapid, automatic, and unconscious response to a stimulus that often protects the body from danger.

RELAY NEURON
A type of neuron that relays nerve impulses from one neuron to another and also processes information.

RIBONUCLEIC ACID (RNA)
A substance that copies and translates the coded instructions in DNA to make proteins.

SENSORY NEURON
A type of neuron that carries nerve impulses from sensory receptors to the central nervous system.

SKELETAL MUSCLE
A type of muscle that is attached to bones and moves the body.

SMOOTH MUSCLE
A type of muscle found in the wall of hollow organs that, for example, pushes urine out of the bladder.

SPECIES
A group of living things that can breed together.

STARCH
A complex carbohydrate produced by plants that, when eaten, is digested into glucose.

STEM CELL
An unspecialized cell that divides repeatedly, giving rise to specialized cells such as muscle or nerve cells.

SYSTOLE
The part of the heartbeat sequence when either the ventricles or the atria are contracted.

TENDON
A cord or sheet of tough connective tissue that connects a muscle to a bone.

TISSUE
A group of one type, or similar types, of cells that work together to perform a particular function.

TRILLION
A number equal to one million million (1,000,000,000,000).

VIRUS
One of a group of infectious non-living agents that cause diseases such as flu and measles.

VITAMIN
One of over 13 substances, including vitamin D, that are needed in small amounts in the diet for normal body functioning.

Index

Acknowledgments

DK would like to thank:
Balloon Art Studio for the cell-division balloons on pages 16–17; Chris Bernstein for preparing the index.

The publisher would like to thank the following for their kind permission to reproduce their photographs:

Key: a–above; b–below/bottom; c–center; f–far; l–left; r–right; t–top

4 Science Photo Library: Steve Gschmeissner (tl); David Mccarthy (tr). **5 Science Photo Library:** Steve Gschmeissner (cl). **6–7 Science Photo Library:** Steve Gschmeissner. **8 Getty Images:** Sue Flood (clb); Shuji Kobayashi (bl); Sergio Pitamitz (cr); Juan Silva (ca). **8–9 iStockphoto.com:** UteHil (c). **9 Dreamstime.com:** Akhilesh Sharma (bl). **Getty Images:** Jurgen Freund (crb); Image Source (cl); Ariadne Van Zandbergen (tc). **iStockphoto.com:** altaykaya (cr); eurobanks (br). **10 Alamy Images:** Encyclopaedia Britannica / Universal Images Group Limited (tr) (bc). **iStockphoto.com:** Hans Slegers (br/Ferns). **Science Photo Library:** Mauricio Anton (cl) (br). **10–11 Getty Images:** Panoramic Images (Background); Thinkstock (fern). **iStockphoto.com:** Dmitry Mordvintsev (c). **11 Alamy Images:** Encyclopaedia Britannica / Universal Images Group Limited (tl). **Getty Images:** The Bridgeman Art Library / Prehistoric (clb). **The Natural History Museum, London:** John Sibbick (ca) (crb). **12 Corbis:** Science Photo Library/ Steve Gschmeissner (bl); Visuals Unlimited (clb) (cb). **13 Science Photo Library:** Eye Of Science (cr); Eric Grave (tc); Steve Gschmeissner (bc); David Mccarthy (bl); Professors P.M. Motta, P.M. Andrews, K.R. Porter & J. Vial (cl). **14 Corbis:** Image Source (fcra). **iStockphoto.com:** Kate Leigh (tr/button). **Science Photo Library:** JJP / Eurelios (cb); Pasieka (tc). **14–15 Dreamstime.com:** Tanikewak (t/balls of wool). **iStockphoto.com:** Laura Eisenberg (t/needles); Magdalena Kucova (b/tape); Tomograf (background). **15 Corbis:** MedicalRF.com (fcl). **iStockphoto.com:** Kate Leigh (tl/button). **Science Photo Library:** Dr. Tony Brain (cl); Equinox Graphics (fcla); Pasieka (fcr). **17 Dorling Kindersley:** Lindsey Stock (tr) (bl). **18 Corbis:** Photo Quest Ltd/ Science Photo Library (cl). **Science Photo Library:** Eye Of Science (bc); Susumu Nishinaga (tc). **18–19 Dorling Kindersley:** Denoyer-Geppert (c). **19 Science Photo Library:** Steve Gschmeissner (br). **20–21 Alamy Images:** Eschcollection L (Background). **21 Science Photo Library:** Steve Gschmeissner (tc). **22 Science Photo Library:** (cb); David M. Martin, MD (tr); Mehau Kulyk (cra); Sovereign, ISM (bl) (cla); Zephyr (br). **23 Science Photo Library:** GJLP (tl); Dr Najeeb Layyous (cr); Hank Morgan (c) (tr); Geoff Tompkinson (br); Zephyr (clb). **24 Corbis:** Owen Franken (cra/beach); Jack Hollingsworth / Blend Images (tc/people); MedicalRF.com (c). **Dreamstime.com:** Marylooo (tr). **iStockphoto.com:** Lyudmyla Nesterenko (fcl). **24–25 Corbis:** Lawrence Manning (background). **25 Corbis:** Miles / Zefa (tc/hands) (ca/jar); Photodisc / Kutay Tanir (c). **Getty Images:** Photodisc / Thomas Northcut (cb/jar) (fbr); Visuals Unlimited / Wolf Fahrenbach (cl). **Science Photo Library:** Martin Dohrn (cb/skin). **26 Corbis:** MedicalRF.com (br). **iStockphoto.com:** Jeff Chevrier (b/Hair on floor); Ronald N Hohenhaus (fbl); Kriando Design (cr); Sefaoncul (fcr); Studiovitra (c). **Science Photo Library:** Susumu Nishinaga (cl); Andrew Syred (bl). **26–27 Alamy Images:** Keith Van-Loen (bc). **iStockphoto.com:** Jerry Mcelroy (tc/Mirror); Alexey Stiop (b/Tiled floor); Xyno (tc/Frame). **27 Alamy Images:** ClassicStock (ftr). **Corbis:** MedicalRF.com (c). **Getty Images:** Tay Jnr (tr); Ralf Nau (tc). **iStockphoto.com:** Hype Photography (cr); Bradley Mason (clb); Overprint (cl); Spiderbox Photography Inc. (cla). **Science Photo Library:** Gustoimages (tl). **28 Getty Images:** Dr. David Phillips (cl). **iStockphoto.com:** 270770 (bl); L. Brinck (bc); Creative Shot (clb); Davincidig (fcl); Brian Pamphilon (fbl); Jon D. Patton (cla); Yuri Shirokov (crb); Vladimir (c). **Science Photo Library:** Martin Dohrn (clb); Eye Of Science (cb); Steve Gschmeissner (br); Andrew Syred (c/Follicle mites). **28–29 Dreamstime.com:** Robert Mizerek (bc). **iStockphoto.com:** Enjoy Industries (Passport stamps); D.J Gunner (cb). **29 Corbis:** David Scharf/ Science Faction (cl). **iStockphoto.com:** Ever (br); Onceawitkin (clb/Immigration stamp); Yuri Shirokov (cb/Pink passport pages); Stokes Design Project (crb); J. Webb (cr). **Science Photo Library:** Eye Of Science (clb); K.H. Kjeldsen (cb); Photo Insolite Realite (fcl). **30–31 Corbis:** Ariel Skelley (t). **iStockphoto.com:** Kirza (t/Photo frame); Christian J. Stewart (b). **31 iStockphoto.com:** Petre Plesea (cr). **32–33 iStockphoto.com:** Morton Photographic (Blackboard). **34 Getty Images:** 3DClinic (tc/sperm); Steve Gschmeissner / SPL (bc); Stone / Yorgos Nikas (cr). **34–35 Corbis:** MedicalRF.com (c). **iStockphoto.com:** Mark Evans (gender symbols). **35 Science Photo Library:** Christian Darkin (tr); Hybrid Medical Animation (crb). **36 Science Photo Library:** Dr M.A. Ansary (c); BSIP, Kretz Technik (tr); Dopamine (cla); Edelmann (tl) (bc). **36–37 Science Photo Library:** Edelmann (bc). **37 Corbis:** MedicalRF.com (cb). **Getty Images:** Christopher Furlong (tr/Photo). **iStockphoto.com:** Archidea Photo (tr). **Science Photo Library:** Neil Bromhall (cl). **38 Dreamstime.com:** Newlight (bc); Picturephoto (ca) (bl). **Getty Images:** Scott E. Barbour (cr). **Science Photo Library:** Scott Camazine (cb). **39 Dreamstime.com:** Newlight (tc); Picturephoto (tl) (cl) (tr). **Getty Images:** Rebecca Emery (crb). **iStockphoto.com:** Jamesmcq24 (cr); Monkey Business Images (tl); Pamspix (bl). **40–41 Science Photo Library:** David Mccarthy. **42 Corbis:** Image Source (c); MedicalRF.com (br); Adrianna Williams (cr). **42–43 Getty Images:** Photodisc / Siede Preis (t). **iStockphoto.com:** Evgeny Kuklev. **43 Dreamstime.com:** Herrherrma... (r/book). **iStockphoto.com:** Kristian Sekulic (r/children). **Science Photo Library:** Scott Camazine (cl); Roger Harris (cra) (crb). **44 Dreamstime.com:** Wd2007 (bc). **iStockphoto.com:** Graffizone (tl); Kelly McLaren (tr). **Science Photo Library:** Susumu Nishinaga (bl); Prof. P. Motta / Dept. Of Anatomy / University "La Sapienza", Rome (ca); Andrew Syred (ftl). **44–45 iStockphoto.com:** Andrew DeCrocker (background). **45 Corbis:** Moodboard (bc); David Scharf / Science Faction (cr). **iStockphoto.com:** Leslie Elieff (tl); Heidijpix (ftr); Tempuraslightbulb (bl). **Science Photo Library:** Robert Becker / Custom Medical Stock Photo (ftl); Paul Gunning (cra). **46 Dorling Kindersley:** The Natural History Museum, London. **Dreamstime.com:** Brad Calkins (fcl); Bruno Sinnah (cl). **47 Alamy Images:** Encyclopaedia Britannica / Universal Images Group Limited (cr). **Corbis:** MedicalRF.com (fcla) (cla); Norbert Schaefer (br). **Dreamstime.com:** Feng Yu / Devonyu (t). **Getty Images:** Photodisc / TRBfoto (clb); Visuals Unlimited / Ralph Hutchings (tl). **48 iStockphoto.com:** James McQuillan (ca). **48–49 iStockphoto.com:** Selahattin Bayram (joints wood texture); Mike Clarke (t); Scubabartek (c/nails); Dave White (b). **49 Corbis:** Roger Tidman (cra). **Dreamstime.com:** Nikolai Sorokin (tl). **iStockphoto.com:** Tom Lewis (cla). **50 Corbis:** Bettmann / Myron (bl); Photo Quest Ltd / Science Photo Library (br). **Getty Images:** The Bridgeman Art Library / Alessandro Algardi (cr). **Science Photo Library:** Prof. S. Cinti (fbr). **50–51 Dreamstime.com:** Kevin Tietz. **iStockphoto.com:** Jochen Miksch (b). **51 Corbis:** Jack Hollingsworth (l). **Getty Images:** AFP Photo / David Boily (tr). **iStockphoto.com:** DNY59 (cb) (br). **Science Photo Library:** Steve Gschmeissner (fbl). **52 Corbis:** Photo Quest Ltd / Science Photo Library (tr) (tr/screen). **Dreamstime.com:** Almir1968 (ca/screen). **52-53 Alamy Images:** Robert Stainforth. **53 Corbis:** MedicalRF.com (tc) (tc/screen) (tr/screen). **Dreamstime.com:** Almir1968 (tl/screen). **Science Photo Library:** Don Fawcett (tl). **54 Corbis:** Alinari Archives / Andrea del Sarto / Fratelli Alinari (cr). **Dreamstime.com:** Cecilia Lim (br). **iStockphoto.com:** Bart Broek (ftr); Roberto A. Sanchez (l); Baris Simsek (bl). **54–55 Dreamstime.com:** Siloto (cb); Trentham (c). **iStockphoto.com:** Kristen Johansen; Wei Ti Ng (b). **55 Corbis:** Visuals Unlimited (cl). **Getty Images:** Photographer's Choice / Frank Whitney (br). **iStockphoto.com:** Jan Rihak (br/pad); Baris Simsek (bl) (fbr); Wei Ti Ng (t). **Science Photo Library:** Roger Harris (tr) (c). **56 Corbis:** Jack Carroll / Icon SMI (bc); Duane Osborn / Somos Images (tr). **Dreamstime.com:** Aleksandar Ljesic (cr); Richard Mcguirk (bc/towels). **iStockphoto.com:** Chris Scredon (ca/masking tape). **56–57 Dreamstime.com:** Jon Helgason. **57 Dreamstime.com:** Nikolai Sorokin (bl). **Getty Images:** The Image Bank / Terje Rakke (c); Jamie McDonald (tl); Stone / Mike Powell (bc). **iStockphoto.com:** DNY59 (t); Tjanze (c/bottle); TommL (fcra). **58 Getty Images:** Marili Forastieri / Photodisc (cl); Jonathan Ford / The Image Bank (clb); Cary Wolinsky / Aurora (cr). **58–59 Dreamstime.com:** Jasenka (ca); Viktor Penner (b). **Getty Images:** Nick White / Digital Vision (bc) (c). **59 Corbis:** Image100 (fclb); MedicalRF.com (clb). **Getty Images:** Aurelie and Morgan David / Cultura (c); Domino / Photodisc (fcrb). **60 Corbis:** MedicalRF.com (tl). **Science Photo Library:** Steve Gschmeissner (cr). **60–61 Corbis:** MedicalRF.com (t). **Getty Images:** Matt Cardy / Getty Images News. **61 Corbis:** Brooke Fasani / Comet (tr); MedicalRF.com (c). **Science Photo Library:** BSIP, Chassenet (tc). **62 iStockphoto.com:** DSGpro (fcl). **Science Photo Library:** Steve Gschmeissner (fcr); Manfred Kage (cr). **62–63 iStockphoto.com:** DSGpro (c); Rype Arts (Icons on screens). **63 iStockphoto.com:** DSGpro (cr) (fcrb). **Science Photo Library:** David M. Phillips / The Population Council (fcl); Dr John Zajicek (cl); Eye Of Science (cra); Steve Gschmeissner (crb). **64 Dreamstime.com:** Picsfive (cl/paper). **iStockphoto.com:** Stefan Nielsen (br); PeJo29 (b). **64–65 Barcroft Media Ltd.:** Karen Norberg (c). **66 Corbis:** Somos (tl); Visuals Unlimited (bl). **Science Photo Library:** Eye Of Science (c); Kent Wood (cb). **66–67 iStockphoto.com:** Fotocrisis (Background). **67 Corbis:** Ale Ventura / PhotoAlto (cb). **Science Photo Library:** BSIP Astier (br). **68 Alamy Images:** Third cross (cr) (bc) (l). **Corbis:** Duncan Smith / Comet (bc/cyclist). **Dreamstime.com:** Nikolay Okhitin (bl). **Science Photo Library:** Arthur Toga / UCLA (ca). **68–69 Alamy Images:** Third cross (b) (c). **Getty Images:** Iconica / Gazimal (t). **69 Corbis:** Edith Held / Fancy (fcra); Image Source (fcrb); Stretch Photography / Blend Images (fcr). **Dreamstime.com:** Roman Borodaev (fcl); Melinda Fawver (cl); X2asompi (bl). **Getty Images:** Jeffrey Coolidge / Photodisc (ftr); Image Source (tl); Vera Storman / Riser (bl/big wheel). **70 Alamy Images:** Danny Bird (bc). **Getty Images:** The Image Bank / Jonathan Kirn (tr). **iStockphoto.com:** Miralex (tr/screen). **Science Photo Library:** BSIP VEM (tl). **71 Corbis:** Allana Wesley White (bl). **Getty Images:** Halfdark (bl/screen); Photographer's Choice / Stephen Simpson (r). **72 Dreamstime.com:** Rachwal (br/lens case). **Getty Images:** 3D4Medical.com (clb); Brand X Pictures (tr); Laurence Monneret / Stone (cla); Photodisc / Thomas Northcut (fbr/glasses); Workbook Stock / Robert Llewellyn (cr). **iStockphoto.com:** Svetlana Larina (clb/frame); Dave White (cl/frame). **73 Getty Images:** 3D4Medical.com (br). **iStockphoto.com:** Marc Fischer (cr); Susan Trigg (tl/frame). **Science Photo Library:** Ralph Eagle (tl); Jacopin (bl); Omikron (cra). **74 Alamy Images:** Frank Geisler / Medicalpicture (bc). **Getty Images:** Nucleus Medical Art, Inc. (tl). **Science Photo Library:** Steve Gschmeissner (c); Susumu Nishinaga (tr). **74–75 Dreamstime.com:** Николай Григорьев / Grynold (c). **75 Corbis:** Joe McDonald (br). **Dreamstime.com:** 001001100dt (c). **Getty Images:** Image Source (tr). **iStockphoto.com:** Mike Bentley (r). **76 Science Photo Library:** Mark Miller (c). **76–77 Corbis:** Bloomimage (c). **iStockphoto.com:** Stacey Newman (background); Skip O'Donnell. **77 Science Photo Library:** Eric Grave (c); Prof. P. Motta / Dept. Of Anatomy / University "La Sapienza", Rome (crb). **78 Corbis:** Steve Gschmeissner / Science Photo Library (ca); Moodboard (bc). **Getty Images:** Michael Blann / Digital Vision (tr); Photonica / David Zaitz (l). **Science Photo Library:** Anatomical Travelogue (cra); Prof. P. Motta / Dept. Of Anatomy / University "La Sapienza", Rome (bc) (cb). **78–79 Dreamstime.com:** Podius (menu). **79 Dreamstime.com:** Peter Kim. **iStockphoto.com:** Marek Mnich (t). **80 iStockphoto.com:** Nickilford (bl). **81 Alamy Images:** Frank Geisler / medicalpicture (bc). **Corbis:** Mario Castello / Fancy (cr). **Getty Images:** Tom Grill / Iconica (tr). **Science Photo Library:** Anatomical Travelogue (tc) (c) (ca) (cb). **82 Corbis:** MedicalRF.com (cr). **Getty Images:** Nucleus Medical Art.com (tc). **Science Photo Library:** Roger Harris (bl); Zephyr (tl). **82–83 Dreamstime.com:** Marinini (ripples); Mtr (test tubes). **Science Photo Library:** Anatomical Travelogue (b). **83 Getty Images:** 3D4Medical.com (tl). **Science Photo Library:** Anatomical Travelogue (ca) (cl). **84 Corbis:** Jay Dickman (cra/roller coaster). **Dreamstime.com:** Jgroup (tr). **iStockphoto.com:** futureimage (br); Jeff Hower (tl); Paul Mckeown (bl). **Science Photo Library:** John Bavosi (cl); Roger Harris (bl/kidneys) (cb). **84–85 iStockphoto.com:** Dan Moore (background). **85 Corbis:** Dr. Richard Kessel & Dr. Randy Kardon / Tissues & Organs / Visuals Unlimited (bl); MedicalRF.com (tl) (cl) (cla). **Dreamstime.com:** Gabor2100 (tr). **iStockphoto.com:** Jan Doddy (br). **86–87 Science Photo Library:** Steve Gschmeissner. **88 Corbis:** Dennis Kunkel Microscopy, Inc./Visuals Unlimited (br). **iStockphoto.com:** Kativ (ca). **Science Photo Library:** Animate4.Com (ca/haemoglobin). **88–89 iStockphoto.com:** Henrik Jonsson (red blood cells). **89 Corbis:** Dennis Kunkel Microscopy, Inc./Visuals Unlimited (br). **90–91 Alamy Images:** Stuart Kelly. **Science Photo Library:** Pasieka (c). **92 Dreamstime.com:** Grybaz (bc); Jezper (background); Picturephoto (c/tools). **Getty Images:** 3D4Medical.com (crb). **92–93 Dreamstime.com:** Frenta (fingerprints); Luminis (b). **iStockphoto.com:** Don Bayley. **93 Alamy Images:** Joachim Lomoth / medicalpicture (br). **Corbis:** JGI / Blend Images (fcl); Radius Images (cl). **Getty Images:** 3D4Medical.com (c); Car Culture (engine). **94 Corbis:** MedicalRF.com (tr) (crb). **iStockphoto.com:** Robert Dant (cra). **94–95 iStockphoto.com:** Adventure_Photo; Nemanja Pesic (bag). **95 Corbis:** MedicalRF.com (clb) (crb). **iStockphoto.com:** TommL (r/hands). **96 Getty Images:** Darryl Leniuk (crb); Bryn Lennon (tr); David Young-Wolff (br). **96–97 Getty Images:** Tetra Images (background). **97 Corbis:** Visuals Unlimited (b). **Getty Images:** Kennan Harvey (t). **98–99 iStockphoto.com:** craftvision (background). **99 Corbis:** JGI / Jamie Grill / Blend Images (cr); MedicalRF.com (tl). **Getty Images:** Michael Krasowitz (bc). **100 Getty Images:** Purestock (tl). **iStockphoto.com:** Graffizone (l) (clb) (cb). **Science Photo Library:** CNRI (bl); Sovereign, ISM (br). **100–101 Getty Images:** Photographer's Choice / Peter Dazeley. **101 Getty Images:** Digital Vision (cr); Photodisc / Flashfilm (tr). **iStockphoto.com:** Graffizone (b); Geoffrey Holman (tc); Luminis (cra). **Science Photo Library:** CNRI (tl). **102–103 Dreamstime.com:** Weknow (Table cloth). **Science Photo Library:** Maximilian Stock Ltd (c). **103 Alamy Images:** Bon Appetit/ Feig (tc). **104 Dreamstime.com:** Alexander Ivanov (tr); Monkey Business Images (cra). **Science Photo Library:** Mark Miller (br). **104–105 Alamy Images:** CoverSpot (c/Inside mouth). **Getty Images:** Andersen Ross (tc). **105 Dreamstime.com:** Nastya81 (tc); Stepan Popov (fbl); Jonathan Souza (bl). **106 Corbis:** MedicalRF.com (bc). **Getty Images:** DK Stock / Christina Kennedy (crb). **106–107 Getty Images:** UpperCut Images. **107 Alamy Images:** Paddy McGuinness (ca). **Corbis:** MedicalRF.com (cr). **Dorling Kindersley:** Denoyer-Geppert (br). **108 Dreamstime.com:** Michael Flippo (bl); Pdtnc (clb); Photobunny (cr). **Getty Images:** Ralph Hutchings (tc). **iStockphoto.com:** Dial-a-view (br); MBPHOTO, INC. (tr). **Science Photo Library:** A. Dowsett, Health Protection Agency (cb). **108–109 iStockphoto.com:** Spiderbox Photography Inc. (Background). **109 Dreamstime.com:** Photobunny (cl) (cr). **iStockphoto.com:** Shantell (tr); Steve Cash Photography (c). **Science Photo Library:** Steve Gschmeissner (clb); Prof. P. Motta / Dept. Of Anatomy / University "La Sapienza", Rome (crb). **110 Science Photo Library:** Brian Evans (clb); Bo Veisland (cl). **110–111 Getty Images:** Nicholas Rigg (Glassware). **111 Getty Images:** Camilla Sjodin (crb). **Science Photo Library:** Alain Pol, ISM (clb). **112 iStockphoto.com:** Duckycards (tl) (bl) (br) (fbr) (ftr) (tr). **Science Photo Library:** BSIP, Cavallini James (cra); Eye Of Science (br); NIBSC (cl). **112–113 iStockphoto.com:** DeGrie Photo Illustration (Background); Fidelio Photography. **113 iStockphoto.com:** Duckycards (tr) (bc) (br). **Science Photo Library:** Dr. Tony Brain (tl); Eye Of Science (c) (cra); Power and Syred (fbr); David Scharf (bl). **114 Corbis:** Clouds Hill Imaging Ltd. (cr). **Dreamstime.com:** Gummy231 (bl). **iStockphoto.com:** Arena Creative (fcl); Richard Laurence (ca); stevedesign.ca (cr); Xyno (cb/Barrier). **Science Photo Library:** Steve Gschmeissner (cb); Science Source (clb). **114–115 Dreamstime.com:** Timurd (t). **iStockphoto.com:** Xyno (c). **115 Corbis:** Photo Quest Ltd/ Science Photo Library (tr). **Dreamstime.com:** Gummy231 (br). **iStockphoto.com:** Arena Creative (fcr); Richard Laurence (ca); stevedesign.ca (cr); Xyno (cb/Barrier). **Science Photo Library:** CNRI (cb); Steve Percival (c); D. Phillips (crb); Professors P. Motta & F. Carpino / Univer- Sity "La Sapienza", Rome (cr). **116 National Cancer Institute / U.S. National Institute of Health / www.cancer.gov:** (ca). **116–117 Alamy Images:** StockImages. **117 Corbis:** MedicalRF.com (fcr). **Dreamstime.com:** Karammiri (cr); Ari Sanjaya (br) (tr). **Science Photo Library:** CNRI (fbr); Dr. P. Marazzi (ftr). **118 Corbis:** David Scharf/ Science Faction (cla); Photo Quest Ltd / Science Photo Library (crb). **Science Photo Library:** Dr Andrejs Liepins (tr). **118–119 iStockphoto.com:** Lisa Valder Photography (Background). **119 Getty Images:** Somos/Veer (cb). **Science Photo Library:** Juergen Berger (cra); Dr Tim Evans (tl). **120 Getty Images:** Blue Jean Images (clb). **iStockphoto.com:** Juliya Shumskaya (tr). **121 Corbis:** HBSS (cr). **Getty Images:** Wayne H Chasan (clb); Carlos de Andres (cl); UpperCut Images (br); Paul Taylor. **iStockphoto.com:** 350jb (tr). **122 iStockphoto.com:** ShyMan (fcl). **Press Association Images:** Brian Walker/ AP (cr). **Science Photo Library:** Antonia Reeve (cl); Sovereign, ISM (ca). **122–123 Getty Images:** Adam Friedberg. **iStockphoto.com:** Dandanian (Boxes); Fckuen (Pallets). **123 Dreamstime.com:** Julián Rovagnati (fcrb). **Getty Images:** Kallista Images (clb). **iStockphoto.com:** GoodMood Photo (clb/Boxes). **Reuters:** Jason Reed (cr). **Science Photo Library:** James King-Holmes (cb); Professor Miodrag Stojkovic (cl)

All other images © Dorling Kindersley
For further information see:
www.dkimages.com